No Regrets

Alexandra Swann

Cygnet Press, El Paso, Texas

Copyright © 1989 by Alexandra Swann.
Published in the U.S.A. by Cygnet Press, Anthony, New Mexico.
First printing, October 1989
Second printing, July 1994
ISBN #09623611-0-0

I shall be telling this with a sigh
Somewhere ages and ages hence:
Two roads diverged in a wood, and I - -
I took the one less traveled by,
And that has made all the difference.

Robert Frost

When I was
five years old.

The month I began
school: Left to right,
Back row: me at age
five, Dad, Christopher
at four.
Front row: Francesca at
three, Dominic at
one year.

ONE
DECISIONS

One month before my fifth birthday my mother began to teach me to read and write, and school at home became a wonderful thing. Our classes were not those of the traditional mother teaching her small daughter letters, shapes, and colors in preparation for kindergarten, however. Unlike most mothers, mine had made a decision to educate me at home. She and I were engaged in serious business, and we knew it. Each day at eight-thirty A.M. our session began, and together the disciplined young mother and her exuberant child explored the mysteries of the alphabet, phonics, writing, addition, and subtraction. She could not have known then -- a twenty-nine year old woman with no previous teaching experience struggling to educate her oldest child with methods she herself had devised -- that only eleven years later she would be called as an expert witness to testify for home-schoolers in *Leeper vs. Arlington*, the landmark court case which would legalize home-schooling in the state of Texas. Yet, even then she possessed the spirit of determination and self-sacrifice which would later earn her that status.

My parents had known even during their first seven childless years of marriage that if they ever did have children, those children would not attend a public school. They had witnessed both the academic and spiritual breakdown of America's classrooms, and they agreed that no child of theirs would be educated in such a system. Within months after their wedding they had decided that they would opt for a private or parochial school which stressed both academics and fundamental Christian values.

However, eleven years later, when I was four years old, they discovered that finding a private institution which would meet their standards was not an easy task. For one thing, at that time there were only a handful of private schools in our area, and none of these was affiliated with our religious denomination. Of these facilities only one -- an Episcopal day school -- met the academic standards that they had hoped to find. Yet, because it offered the best educational facilities and because my parents felt that attendance there would provide some protection from corrupting influences, they decided that they would send me to St. Clements.

Because of its outstanding reputation in the community, St. Clements had a waiting list of more than a year for new students. Therefore, my father agreed to make an appointment for an interview so that he could have my name placed on the list for the kindergarten the following year. However, the night before he was to make that call my mother had a dream, and that dream would permanently change our lives.

In her dream, Mother was sitting in a chair with an open Bible in her lap. Written across the pages of the Old Testament in words of fire was the message, "Do not send the children to school, lest they be corrupted." She then turned to the New Testament where the same fiery script appeared. This time the message read, "For My wisdom is sufficient."

Mother was very disturbed by this dream, and in the morning she shared it with my father. As they began to ponder its meaning, they decided that they would postpone the call to St. Clements. If this dream were from God, He must have a special plan for the education of their children, and they wanted to make certain that they follow the leading of His Spirit.

The first thing that puzzled them was the mandate not to send the children to school "lest they be corrupted." My parents were certain that God did not want their children to be uneducated. They knew that God possesses all knowledge and all wisdom. For a child to remain ignorant cannot possibly glorify Him; therefore, they felt that the key to educating their children lay in finding a method of instruction that would not corrupt.

First, Mother researched the word "corruption." She found that The American Heritage Dictionary defines corrupt as, "immoral, perverted, depraved, marked by venality and dishonesty, decaying, putrid, impure, contaminated, and unclean." Nothing new here. But further down the list she saw something that caught her eye, "to change the original form of." That was it! Yes, if the Lord had indeed spoken to her, he was cautioning her against all the familiar pitfalls associated with corruption, but he was saying something else equally important. If her children were mainstreamed into the system, they would be "changed" -- changed from the beings He had created. They might even be changed to such a degree that they would never find their way back to those individuals that He had created. They might never be able to perform the work He had for them. Her children had a mission in life, but for them to accomplish this work they must not be changed.

The second part of the dream was even more frustrating: "For My wisdom is sufficient." What could that mean? Was God commanding them to teach their children only the scriptures and things relating to the church? Surely not.

As Mother and Dad searched for answers, they began to discover certain inaccuracies in their concept of God. They believed that God is all powerful and all wise. They were absolutely certain that there is nothing He cannot do. Yet, somehow, they viewed Him as a sort of "simple primitive" not unlike the character portrayed by Charlton Heston in *The Ten Commandments*. They had never envisioned Him as a being concerned with technology, the sciences and the humanities. It was only when they started to view God as the God of the computer chip and the laser that they began to understand what His wisdom really encompassed. Rather than telling them not to educate their children, He was leading them into a more perfect method of instruction. My parents finally came to realize that in order to be obedient they must provide their children with the finest education that is available in today's world, but they must also find a way to do this without putting them in a traditional classroom.

At the time that my parents made their decision to tutor me, the home-schooling movement as we know it today did not exist. We knew of no home-school support groups nor did home-schoolers receive national attention in the media. Mother had heard of only one family who had attempted to teach their own children, and they were traveling Mennonite missionaries who home-schooled with moderate success. Consequently, her family and friends were shocked by her decision, and many said that she could not possibly succeed. In fact, both sets of in-laws were violently opposed to the idea. She was told that children can learn only when taught by "real" teachers. People assured her that children cannot learn from their parents because they will not respond well. Skeptical friends informed her that she not only would not teach me anything, but that she might actually damage me so that I could not learn from anyone else.

All of these fatalistic predictions were very discouraging and made her decision all the more difficult, for they echoed her own apprehensions. Still, she and my father were determined to at least attempt home-schooling. In order to allay some of her own fears, Mother reasoned as follows: (1) Initially, I would be enrolled in the first grade. She had attended and graduated from the first grade, and she felt certain that she still possessed first grade skills. Therefore, she should certainly be able to pass those skills on to me. (2) She would begin by attempting to teach me to read, for if she were not capable of teaching me to read, obviously she would not be able to teach me anything else. If, on the other hand, she were successful, she might be able to teach me other skills as well. (3) I was not quite five years old. Even if she proved totally incapable of teaching me anything during the next two years, I could still be enrolled in a private school at age seven without any time having been lost from my education.

On the day that I began school, Mother had four children under the age of five years, and she was pregnant with her fifth. Her average day was divided among the various responsibilities of taking care of her house, raising her children, preparing meals, and tutoring me. She soon found that she no longer had time for telephone chats, visits with friends, or luncheons. Every waking moment was consumed either by her household duties or by the academic experiment upon which she had embarked.

As for me, I was aware neither of the sacrifices nor the effort, but only that I was engaged in a mature, delightful endeavor. Each day new wonders unfolded before me. Almost immediately I learned to print my name, and soon I was able to communicate on paper. Not only could I write words, but I could also write numerals from one to one hundred. The one-hundred addition and subtraction tables were becoming second nature. I could even tell time. However, none of these feats rivaled my greatest accomplishment -- learning to read.

It has been said that teachers often succeed in making children hate reading while trying to teach them to do so. It appears that many children associate reading with errors and humiliation because they are required to read difficult books aloud in front of the entire class. When the child stumbles or cannot pronounce a word properly, the class laughs, and the teacher may ask him to "try again." The poor child feels like a fool and soon begins to avoid reading as a way of avoiding mistakes.

Learning to read was not at all traumatic for me, primarily because of the way in which I was taught. Mother did not use a sight reading program but instead stressed phonics. She began by teaching me to recognize the consonants and to pronounce the sounds made by each. Next, she taught me to identify the vowels and to pronounce their long and short sounds. Then she taught me the different vowel-consonant combinations and how to use the combinations to form words. For example, if I know that the letters "a-n" are pronounced "an," then the letters "r-a-n" must form the word "ran." Within a short time, I could read such simple books as *Hop on Pop* and *The Cat in the Hat.* She and I worked alone together each day, and she patiently corrected my mistakes without making me feel foolish. Her praise was warm and frequent, and it always encouraged me to step up my efforts and work still harder. Thus, for me, learning to read was a very pleasant experience, and the love for books and reading which I developed during those early weeks has lasted.

Yet, the day came for me, as it does for most children, when the glow began to fade, the novelty wore off, and I no longer found school enchanting. I was prepared to become the world's youngest dropout. Upon announcing my intention, I was confronted with a side of my teacher I had not previously seen -- the stern, disciplinarian side I often encountered in ordinary life when I refused to do as I was told. Gently but firmly Mother explained that school was not optional. I was required to attend and complete my lessons in a satisfactory manner -- I had no choice. We doubtless had a scene which resulted in my shedding a few tears, but in the end the teacher stood victorious and the mutiny was quashed. The incident was the first of several minor confrontations which would serve to establish dominance over the class, and I soon found that it was Mother's dominance that was being established. One of the most important lessons I would learn in school would be to accept her authority over me.

As for Mother, from the very beginning she was firm about school and all things pertaining to it. She understood all too well that without discipline, order, and organization our program did not have a prayer. Even under the best of conditions, the odds against her success were tremendous.

Within a few months, however, the results of this routine became apparent. The experiment was a success; I was indeed learning! Our accomplishments had not just "happened," however -- discipline and dedication had been the keys. The day never came when Mother was too weary, too busy, or too bored to continue with my studies. Neither did the day ever arrive when I was allowed not to study because I was bored or tired. We had an established curriculum which we followed to the letter. It was during those days that the first of many school traditions was established -- I learned what I needed to learn, and what Mother felt I should learn, not necessarily what I wanted to learn.

I quickly adjusted to having my mother as my teacher, and it seemed to be the most natural situation that could exist. When I was studying, she sat next to me, assisting and supervising during our entire session. I wanted her to be proud of me, and I tried very hard to please her -- much harder than I would have tried to please a stranger.

Still, she had her work cut out for her. Though my parents had taught me to be obedient from infancy, they had also pampered me. Consequently, I was accustomed to having my own way much of the time and thought nothing of making outrageous demands. For example, when I was about four years old I decided that the moon was my personal property, and as such it belonged in my bedroom. "It is mine," I claimed, "I know because it follows me home at night." My parents tried to convince me that the request was completely unreasonable, but I stubbornly repeated my demand for several months, until finally I realized that I was not going to receive satisfaction. Mother and Dad had barely succeeded in convincing me that the heavenly bodies belong to everyone when I requested two rather unusual pets -- a giraffe and a mosquito. Mother could understand my interest in the giraffe since they are somewhat exotic creatures, but she never knew the reason for my fascination with the mosquito. Fortunately, children are fickle, and within a few months I had abandoned these ideas in favor of what I considered to be a much less unrealistic gift -- I now wanted a basketful of ladybugs.

Needless to say, I eventually matured beyond making such bizarre requests, but the zany, headstrong personality which had given birth to these notions persisted. One of Mother's most important tasks as my teacher was to curb my stubborn streak. True, she did not wish to "break my spirit," but she did realize that I must be molded into a cooperative, manageable human being. I would have to learn that my every wish could not always be fulfilled, and the classroom seemed as good a place as any to begin the lesson. Sometimes her approach was firm, other times it was gentle, but always it was successful.

Mother understood the various nuances of my personality much better than any stranger might, and she was, thus, able to adapt the tone and technique of her instruction to suit my moods. Of course, I had always responded far better to Mother than to anyone else -- except my father. On the day of my birth, the hospital nurses brought me to her in desperation, complaining that my constant crying was disrupting the entire nursery. While the other newborns were sleeping contentedly, I was squealing my little head off. The moment Mother took me in her arms, though, my crying stopped and I snuggled close to her and went to sleep. Not much had changed in five years -- Mother still had a very soothing effect on me. As a result, we had almost no conflicts, and because we enjoyed such an excellent rapport, our sessions together were very productive.

When I was five years and four months old my parents began to search for a correspondence school through which I could complete the first eight grades. They had planned almost from the day of my birth that eventually I would attend a university and later proceed to graduate work. They believed, however, that if this goal were to be realized, I would have to attend thoroughly accredited elementary and secondary schools, for without the proper credentials I could not hope to gain admittance into a university. Therefore, they were very careful in their choice of an elementary school.

My father contacted his attorney and asked that he help us locate an accredited private school through which I could study in my home. About a week later Mr. Craven called to recommend Calvert School in Baltimore, Maryland. Shortly afterward, my parents were discussing our educational arrangement with a visiting missionary. They told him that they had been looking for an accredited correspondence elementary school, but they did not mention Calvert. Immediately, the missionary advised them to use Calvert School, adding that it is the school used by many church boards with missionaries in parts of the world where conventional schools are either non-existent or inadequate.

Encouraged by this favorable report, my father contacted officials in the state of Maryland and the accrediting association in New York. Both confirmed that Calvert is one of the finest private schools in the world, and representatives in New York added that even if I were to be sent to a boarding school in Switzerland, I would not receive a finer education than at Calvert.

Within the month my father had contacted Calvert about enrolling me; unfortunately, the school officials were hesitant to do so. Although I was five years and four months old -- the minimum age at which Calvert will admit a child to the first grade -- the administrators felt that I would not be mature enough to complete so comprehensive a program. However, after much negotiation they agreed to send me an entrance examination, which I successfully passed. I was then officially enrolled, although the Headmaster cautioned my father that my progress would be carefully monitored.

Calvert's motto is "the school that comes to you." I cannot imagine a more appropriate slogan, for when the course arrives one cannot help feeling that he has been sent everything except the schoolhouse itself. Calvert provides the pupil with books, pencils, paper, rulers, erasers, a compass and protractor if necessary, and in the lower grades a box of Crayola crayons. In addition, it furnishes an instruction manual for the Home Teacher which maps out the pupil's daily lesson plan, provides step-by-step instructions for the administration of the program, and includes tests. Each of these services is provided for the cost of the course. For a small additional fee the student can have the benefit of the advisory teaching service. With the service, he submits each test to the school where it is graded by a teacher and then returned to the pupil. In this way Calvert maintains a complete record of the child's grades. Upon completion of a grade, the student receives a certificate of completion.

Although Calvert expects most of its students to enroll in September and follow a nine-month school year, it is not required that they do so. Students may enroll at any time of the year, and are allowed to progress at their own pace, with up to two years to complete each course. Thus, I began the first grade in February of 1976. Mother immediately saw that I could easily complete several lessons each day, and very soon I was averaging sixteen lessons each week.

Though I was working at a very rapid pace, I never felt tired or overextended. Part of the reason for this was that my schedule was actually very light. Each morning when I came to school I completed my reading and mathematics, which usually took about an hour. Then, Mother called a two hour recess, during which my brother and sister and I played outside. This gave me a chance to unwind, relax and exercise. At eleven-thirty we were called back inside for lunch, which was usually followed by another hour of play. School resumed at one o'clock each afternoon when Mother sat down and helped me finish my lessons. Often my school day lasted no longer than three hours. Further, I had no "homework." All of my lessons were completed during school hours, and the rest of the time was my own.

These three hours were extremely productive, however, because they were devoted strictly to studying. I was not permitted to fidget, play, laugh, sing, or even speak except in connection with my assignment. I had three hours of totally concentrated study time, and in spite of my very young age, I was able to concentrate amazingly well. Although I was considerably younger than the average first grader, I was very mature for my age. Consequently, I was able to perform tasks which would normally be assigned to much older children. For instance, the Calvert first grade manual cautions the Home Teacher against attempting to teach cursive writing to a child under the age of six and a half because his motor skills are not sufficiently developed. However, I learned cursive at the age of five.

Although I was taught at home, or perhaps because of it, Mother strove to make certain that I was very serious about my studies. I took great pride in my accomplishments and was deeply disappointed when I felt I had "fallen short of the mark." I can still observe this attitude among even the youngest children in our family. Recently Gabrielle, who is eight and in the sixth grade, was telling me that she had been very preoccupied that day. "For one thing," she said, "I've been doing terrible in school and I've had that on my mind." (When I later spoke with Mother about it, she told me that actually Gabrielle was doing very well, and she could not imagine why she would be displeased with herself.)

While we were not obsessed with our studies, we were, and are conscientious about them. Mother taught us to set high standards for ourselves. The result was that we became our own toughest critics, working diligently on a project until we felt satisfied with it. This attitude not only improved the quality of our work, it also helped us emotionally. Good grades earned through hard work gave us a tremendous sense of achievement and inspired us to work still harder.

After every twenty lessons I was tested in each subject. Because my parents had opted for the Advisory Teaching Service, the tests were submitted to the school where they were graded. Calvert has a numerical grading system of 1-4 (1 = excellent, 2 = good, 3 = passing, 4 = failing). My first test was returned to me with grades of no lower than 2+ in any subject. In fact, of the 8 tests which I took in the first grade, I scored no lower than 2+ on any.

Within two and a half months I had completed the first grade. It was now early April, and I could have settled into an extended summer vacation. However, Mother believed that the time away from my studies would ultimately be harmful to me, since I would have a tendency to forget much of what I had already learned. Therefore, she promptly enrolled me in the second grade. I, thus, embarked upon a twelve-month school year -- another tradition which continues in our home. I was not required to study on Saturdays or Sundays, and I was given the day off on Christmas, Easter, Thanksgiving, and most federal holidays. In addition, any time I was ill -- which was seldom -- I had the day off. The rule concerning sick leave was that if I were too ill to go to school I could stay in bed. When I became well enough to get up and play, I was well enough to return to my studies.

These were my only vacations. I did not receive two weeks off for Christmas, or spring break, or summer vacation. In fact, I was quite old before I learned that these holidays are observed by most school children.

Though this routine may seem strict, in reality it provided me with an enormous sense of comfort and security. If my routine had been disorganized and haphazard, I might have felt that my life had no direction. Children need constants in their lives, and for many, school is a constant. Whether the school is public or private, they know that they must arrive at a certain time, remain for a certain number of hours, and leave at a certain time. The presence of the studies per se, along with the familiar faces of friends and teachers, can be depended upon.

Though I did not leave my home, I, too, was locked into a dependable routine. Each day I knew that I would rise at a certain hour, begin my studies at a certain time, have recess at a certain time, etc. School was thoroughly reliable -- its presence in my life was a fact which could be counted on five days a week, regardless of whatever else might happen. While I looked forward to a holiday as much as any other child, the basically unvarying schedule provided me with a sense of security and stability.

Because my emotional development was as important to my parents as my intellectual development, they worked hard to teach me respect for other people -- for their accomplishments, talents, and abilities. They were aware that if I continued to progress at the accelerated rate at which I was working, I would find myself far ahead academically of other children my age, and they feared that this might lead to feelings of estrangement. Therefore, they always assured me that while it is true that most five-year-olds are not in the second grade, basically all people are very much alike, and I was really no different from anyone else. "With proper training, any child with average intelligence could accomplish exactly the same thing," Mother has often said. The older that I grow, the more I find this to be true, but even then I realized that while my experiences might be different, I, personally, was very much like all other five-year-olds.

It was my contacts with other children which really "brought this concept home" though. My parents had a number of friends who had children my age with whom I played. One girl of whom I was especially fond was Polly Mills. Polly was seven, the only girl and youngest of five children. She had a clubhouse in her backyard, and she and I spent many happy hours playing there. We were the best of friends until her family moved to Oklahoma.

After Polly left, my parents enrolled me in a ballet class. The teacher was a friend of theirs, and twice a week I took lessons in her home with a class of other little girls. Although I did not meet anyone whom I liked so well as my recently departed chum, I was fond of several of the other girls in the class. Though I was enrolled for only a year before my family moved, it is a period in my life of which I have very pleasant memories.

Finally, perhaps the most stabilizing factor during those early years was my relationship with my family. We have always been very close, and even when we children were small, our happiest hours were the ones we spent together. We had a very nice swing set, and my brother and sister and I spent many wonderful hours playing on it. When the West Texas sun became too warm for such roughhousing, we often climbed the trees which lined the side of our home. We knew we were not supposed to -- Mother had warned us repeatedly of the dangers of tree climbing -- but we did it anyway. My brother Christopher was the most nimble -- I never understood how he could scale to such glorious heights amid the foliage. Francesca was always right on his heels, while I was a bit more timid and did not venture very high. When Mother spotted us, one's position in the tree made no difference anyway -- everyone had to come inside.

In this yard we created our most delightful memories. It was there that we watched our mother kill a rattlesnake with a hoe; there that we played in the tar on the newly paved street -- for which we all got into serious trouble -- and there that Chris perfected his technique for catching birds, toads, and lizards. There we built wonderful castles in the sand and houses under

11

the trees. It was in that yard that we watched beautiful desert sunsets with my father as he watered the lawn. We spent many pleasant evenings taking long walks together or simply playing while my parents looked on.

Although Dad worked during the day, he was home by six o'clock most evenings, giving us the opportunity to have a nice family dinner together. When dinner was finished, he would take us outside where we would help him feed our six calves, who had to be bottle fed because they had been sold apart from their mothers. Every evening, Dad would arm each of us with an enormous bottle filled with formula and lead us to the field. He would then help us get each calf started nursing, and we would hold the bottles until they finished. We looked forward to the ritual, not only because we felt very grown up about getting to stay up past our bedtimes, but also because we enjoyed working with the awkward young calves. We were reminded that this was not play, however, and we had to behave ourselves. I can remember crying on one occasion as I lugged my bottle to the house after being ordered back inside for having misbehaved.

Usually we had a wonderful time with my father, for he is a very lively, colorful person, and he could often suggest the most wonderful projects. Once he decided that since we live on the Mexican border, we needed to learn to speak Spanish. Further, he personally was going to teach us, which promised to be quite a feat considering that he does not speak Spanish himself. He bought a book of beginner's Spanish and copied on note paper for us certain Spanish words and phrases, along with their English translations. Then, every evening for about two weeks, he had us recite the Spanish words and phrases and their English definitions, while he coached our pronunciations. At the time I could not have been more than six or seven years old, and the idea of mastering a foreign language seemed incredibly exciting to me and my younger brothers and sisters. Unfortunately, after a couple of weeks Dad lost interest and canceled the course. We had not learned much Spanish, but we had certainly had a lot of fun trying.

During these years I also developed a wonderful relationship with my mother, which I attribute largely to the fact that she was also my teacher. We undoubtedly spent far more time together than we would have under other circumstances, and this, also, led to feelings of safety and security. During one period my younger siblings and I watched "Captain Kangaroo" every morning before school. The "Captain" closed each show by reminding parents to "spend some time with your young person today." Upon hearing these words, I always glowed with pride at the realization that my parent would be spending the entire day with me.

I was learning to look forward to our sessions together, for Mother had a special talent for making school fun. Often, my enjoyment of my studies was due largely to the cheerful, enthusiastic attitude she projected. I was never allowed to say, "I hate school." School was not merely a duty; it was also intended as a pleasant, interesting activity to be enjoyed and appreciated. Mother did everything in her power to help me learn to love learning. When she read us a story, she did not merely "read" the tale, rather she performed it, assigning each character a different voice and then reading his dialogue accordingly. When she gave us our math assignments, she often preceded the lesson by saying, "This is easy. You're going to think it's a lot of fun." Occasionally, when she knew that we were tired, she would interject a funny comment and make us laugh. She was never simply a teacher; she was also head morale booster.

If the home-school environment were emotionally healthful for me, however, it was emotionally exhausting for Mother. In the second grade, as in the first, she had continued to assign me more than one lesson each day. Consequently, I continued to progress at an accelerated rate. In six months I had completed the second grade, and was ready to be enrolled in the third. Christopher's fifth birthday was approaching, and within a very short time he would be ready to begin school. Panic was setting in. Tutoring one child was difficult and time consuming, and tutoring two seemed nearly impossible. The thought brought her many sleepless nights.

On one of these occasions, as she lay awake turning the situation over in her mind, she was reminded of a story which she and I had read only a few days earlier in school -- "The Keeping of the Bridge." The story retells how ancient Rome was once attacked by an enormous army of Etruscans. The army, which was camped on the opposite bank of the Tiber, had only to cross a narrow wooden bridge to enter the city. Though the Romans hastened to cut down the bridge, it appeared that the enemy soldiers would cross before the bridge had been completely destroyed and the city would be lost. However, living in Rome was a brave soldier named Horatius. Horatius ordered the men of the city to continue cutting down the bridge while he and two other volunteers prevented the enemy from crossing.

To the amusement of the Etruscans, the three took their

places, swords drawn, on the bridge. What the enemy did not realize was that the bridge was so narrow that it could accommodate only three men standing abreast. Therefore, Horatius and his friends had only to fight one man each. By defeating one man at a time, these courageous soldiers were able to hold the bridge until it could be destroyed. At that point, the enemy army, unwilling to build another bridge, returned home.

Mother realized that there was an important lesson to be learned from this story. Had Horatius permitted himself to think of the thousands of soldiers waiting on the shore, he would have concluded that the task was impossible, for three men could never hope to defeat an entire army. However, because of the limited space on the bridge, they, in fact, had to defeat only three men at a time, and this was possible. Mother began to understand that she would have to take the same approach about school. If she allowed herself to look ahead to the many years and many students facing her, she would not have the courage to do even that which she had already begun. Consequently, she adopted a one-day-at-a-time approach, striving each day to complete those tasks immediately ahead of her. She knew that she was capable of teaching one child, for she had been doing so successfully for several months. Therefore, she continued to tutor me without worrying about how she would handle a second student. When the time came for Christopher to be enrolled, she made room in her schedule to teach him also. In this way, she survived the pressure which home-schooling placed on her.

Perhaps the incredible success of her plan gave her a sense of triumph which made the stress more bearable. Within six months I had completed the third grade and was ready to be enrolled in the fourth. I was receiving a wonderful education -- my studies included reading, composition, spelling, arithmetic, mythology, and geography, and I was maintaining excellent grades. It soon became apparent that at this rate I would complete the elementary grades at a younger age than the average child. In fact, Mother felt that it was not unrealistic to expect me to have earned a master's degree by the time I was eighteen, without ever having skipped even one lesson in school.

Christopher also had "come of age" -- he was enrolled in the first grade at Calvert at the age of five years and four months following five months of working privately with Mother. He, too, completed the first grade in two and one half months and was then enrolled in the second grade which he completed in six months. Amazingly, all of the children in our family have begun school at exactly the same age, and progressed through each level at precisely the same rate while maintaining excellent grades, a fact which, I believe, tells a great deal more about our teacher than it does about her students.

The following year, Francesca, who is two and a half years younger than I, began learning to read and write, and after five months was ready to be enrolled in the first grade. Perhaps far off in the dark recesses of her mind, Mother could hear the clashing of steel as the sword of Horatius fought on to victory. For, like her hero, with each passing year she defeated the odds against her own success, and came one step closer to realizing her goal of educating each of her children herself. She now had three students working on three different grade levels, all of whom she taught simultaneously. Though her schedule was physically and emotionally taxing, to her the work and worry were worthwhile.

There was, however, a dark threat looming over us. We lived in the state of Texas, where at that time, the law required not only the compulsory education of all children but the compulsory attendance of all children between the ages of seven years and seventeen years in a public or private classroom.

By the time that I was seven years old, I was enrolled in the fifth grade. It seemed very unreasonable to my parents to have to enroll me in the first grade of a more conventional private school. They believed that I would suffer scholastically and emotionally from such a step, but at the same time they did not want to violate the law by home-schooling illegally. My parents' attorney contacted the state officials on our behalf and requested that we be allowed an exemption from the compulsory attendance law. The officials stood firm, however. If our family remained in Texas, my parents would be forced either to enroll me in school or face prosecution. Unwilling to jeopardize either our family or our education, my parents decided to leave the state.

Because we knew of no state law that explicitly provided for home-schooling, Dad and Mother discussed both Canada and Australia as possible alternatives. They also considered moving to Mississippi, since at that time Mississippi had no compulsory education law. Any of these steps would entail great personal sacrifice, particularly since my father would be required to leave his lucrative employment in El Paso, Texas, and start over somewhere else. While he was willing to do this, it seemed that there should be a way to legally home-school which would not involve such drastic measures.

Finally, after extensive inquiry, we learned that the state of New Mexico had a rather ambiguous law regarding education, and that we might qualify under it as a private school. Our attorney contacted state officials and inquired as to whether we could receive an exemption allowing us to home-school. Senator Frank O. Papen, chairman of the Legislative School Study Committee, responded to our inquiry with a letter from Richard Johnson, director of the Committee, stating that no exemption would be necessary because "A student taking correspondence courses does satisfy the provisions of the Compulsory Attendance Law." A letter from Charles Noland, Assistant General Counsel to the New Mexico Department of Education, further confirmed that because we were enrolled in correspondence courses, we could qualify as a private school and would not need to seek state approval.

Unknown to us, there were a number of other families in Texas who shared our predicament. Many of these chose to remain in the state, and through their vigilance and industry, they were finally successful in bringing a suit against the state which resulted in the legalization of home-schooling in Texas. Their ultimate victory was not without its price, however, for some of these families suffered several years of prosecution and harassment from school boards and local authorities. They were fined, threatened, and dragged into court. While my parents have the greatest respect for these families, they simply felt that it would be to our advantage to leave rather than suffer this type of abuse. They wanted to be able to raise their children with as few complications as possible, and they feared that a serious confrontation with Texas' officials might result in a permanent separation from one another. They were not willing to take that risk.

As El Paso borders New Mexico, the move would not really disrupt our lives. Consequently, with Johnson's and Papen's letters in our possession, we arranged to buy a house across the state line, and on July 4, 1978, our family moved from El Paso, Texas, to Dona Ana County, New Mexico.

TWO
TRANSITIONS

ndependence Day was highly appropriate for our move. Our
exodus to New Mexico had freed us of legal worries and
provided us with the independence to continue our
educations without fear of repercussions. It also marked the
beginning of a new era for us -- an era filled with transitions.
During the years that followed I would make the transition from
elementary school to high school, from high school to college,
and from college to graduate work. I would also leave childhood
behind and enter that difficult period of life known as the "teen
years."

Thirteen days after our move, my parents' sixth child was born
prematurely. Benjamin was only three weeks early, but at birth
he weighed a mere four pounds two ounces. He was too weak
even to nurse, and his lungs were barely strong enough to
supply sufficient oxygen to his body. On the night of his birth
one doctor predicted that he would most certainly die. Because
my parents were well aware of the complications which can
result from placing infants in incubators, they decided to care
for Benji at home. Every day Mother hand-expressed milk from
her breast and then fed it to Benjamin with an eye-dropper.
He was so tiny and frail that he could swallow only one drop
at a time, and even then Mother had to hold his mouth shut
between drops to ensure that he swallowed. It took her forty-
five minutes to give him three-quarters of an ounce of fluid

-- the maximum he would take at one time. The moment he had finished she set her alarm clock to ring in exactly two hours, at which time his next feeding began.

She continued in this way, feeding him every two hours, twenty-four hours a day, for three weeks. As a result of this constant care and attention, he improved rapidly. Though most babies -- even those in hospitals -- experience weight loss after birth, Benjamin never did. During the first week of his life he maintained his birth weight, and after that he gained steadily. At the end of three weeks he was able to nurse normally. Around that time our pastor and his wife visited us, and upon hearing Benjamin fussing in his car bed which Mother had placed near her on the kitchen counter, they asked if we had a new puppy!

While Mother cared for Benjamin and continued to teach us our lessons, she was coping with other distractions as well. Our "new" home was seventy-seven years old, and it required extensive renovation as well as decoration. Over the years the various owners had added rooms without careful planning or consideration. The result was that the house, which has five bedrooms and four baths, had ample floor space but relatively small, dark rooms. Mother and Dad took part of the money from the sale of their previous home and used it to hire carpenters to tear walls down, enlarge rooms, and refinish floors and cabinets. Unfortunately, because we had already sold our other house, we had no choice but to live in this one while it was being renovated. Every morning for months we children completed our lessons with the sounds of drills, saws and hammers accompanying us. Once I sat at our kitchen table studying while, nearby, a carpenter used a power tool. As the harsh sound of the drill became more intense, I had the overwhelming urge to jump from my seat and demand of my mother, "How can you expect me to study in the middle of all this bedlam!"

With the passing months we somewhat adjusted to the noise -- I learned to study and Benjamin learned to sleep without waking. Then, a few weeks before Christmas, the day came for the kitchen to be remodeled. For about a week, Mother had six small mouths to feed and no way to cook, but she responded to the mini crisis with a solution which was not only practical but fun. Every day at lunch time she took all of us to Kentucky Fried Chicken, McDonalds, or Weinerschnitzel. This was a great treat, for we usually ate sandwiches and leftovers for lunch. I was almost sorry when the kitchen was ready to be put back into service, and to this day whenever I think about the house being remodeled, I remember the loss of the kitchen with fondness.

By Christmas the kitchen was nearly finished, and Mother was able to do her holiday cooking. She prepared her traditional homemade fudge and a special nutbread during the week before the holiday. Then, two or three days before Christmas Eve, the carpenters asked us to leave the house for a few hours so that they could lacquer the cabinets. Mother carefully wrapped the candies, and placed them, along with all of the breads and foodstuffs, on our dining table; she covered the table with a cloth to keep the solution from filtering into the food. Then she took us out to lunch while they finished their work. When we returned several hours later, we found that our house reeked. Mother immediately rushed to check our holiday foods, and discovered that in spite of her precautions, all of the breads tasted exactly like lacquer. Even the fudge was ruined! The loss seemed to be a monumental disaster to an eight-year-old, but Mother comforted me and my brothers and sisters and compensated by buying candy for Christmas.

In spite of the many inconveniences brought on by our move, my parents were very pleased that our legal problems with home-schooling had been resolved, for they were delighted with Calvert, and would have deeply regretted our being forced into regular classrooms. After eighty-nine years of service, Calvert School has set such a standard of excellence that children taking placement tests to transfer into Calvert from public or private schools often place several grades below the grade level on which they were working in their previous schools.

Calvert's program is, indeed, designed to provide the pupil with an exceptional education. Beginning in the fourth grade, a day's lesson includes reading, spelling, and mathematics, and usually history, geography, science, grammar, and/or composition. As early as the third grade the pupil studies Greek mythology. History is also introduced in the third grade, beginning with a study of Abraham, Isaac, and Jacob, and continuing through the time of Abraham Lincoln. Even at this stage the child is required to memorize dates and is expected to be able to summarize basic events. From the fourth grade on, American history and world history are alternated, so that each year the student studies one of the two.

Art appreciation also begins early. The second grade course includes color photographs of famous paintings, complete with the name of the painting, the name of the artist, the dates during which he or she lived, the country in which he or she lived, the medium in which the work was painted, and the museum in which the work is now on display. By the end of the course the pupil is expected to be familiar with each of the paintings and the information included about them. Then, in the fifth, sixth, and seventh grades, the child is assigned *A Child's History of Art,* on the respective subjects of painting, sculpture, and architecture which take him from ancient Egyptian art and architecture through that of twentieth-century America. He, thus, becomes familiar with different periods of art and the work of different artists. Even a small child receiving such an education can walk into an art gallery and recognize the names of artists he has studied.

Although all of the subjects in Calvert require that the student spend a great deal of time reading, in addition, he is assigned a daily reading lesson which often includes one or more reading workbooks. As a part of each reading test, the pupil is required to memorize a stanza or two of poetry which he recites to the "Home Teacher." (In the higher grades, he must write the memorized portion himself, capitalizing and punctuating correctly). He is also required to memorize several Psalms.

Finally, as a part of each grade's reading lesson the pupil is assigned several books of stories. Beginning in the third grade, we were assigned books in which we read little known stories of great men, brave soldiers, and heroic deeds -- tales of Robin Hood, King Arthur, William Tell, and El Cid. The stories themselves can almost be considered a study of good citizenship, for many recount the struggles of various countries for freedom from despotic rule, and nearly all stress the virtues of patriotism, courage, wit, determination, and self-sacrifice. They easily excited our imaginations while teaching us some history, for many of the tales are true, and those which are not are deeply rooted in legend.

As we grew older, short stories of romance and adventure were replaced by longer ones. In the higher grades we read *Robinson Crusoe, King Arthur, The Arabian Nights,* and *The Swiss Family Robinson.* Other classics included Charles Dickens' *David Copperfield,* Mark Twain's *The Prince and the Pauper,* Sir Arthur Conan Doyle's *The Hound of the Baskervilles,* Jules Verne's *Around the World in Eighty Days,* and Robert Louis Stevenson's *Kidnapped,* to name a few. Through these works we not only were introduced to some of literature's best known authors, but our reading proficiency and vocabularies were increased.

Because the ability to write well is as important as the ability to read well, starting in the second grade the student may be assigned simple compositions as often as two or three times a week. The manual generally contains a list of possible subjects, some based on recent reading, history, art history, or science lessons. The composition is to be neat -- in the student's finest penmanship -- well worded, and of a specified length -- usually between one-half and one page in the lower grades, between two and two and a half pages in the higher grades. The primary advantage of the composition is that it teaches children to write well and to enjoy writing. It also familiarizes them with the most elementary forms of research. Years later, when I attended the university, I was amazed at how much I relied upon skills I learned in Calvert while preparing my papers. Because in Calvert I was required to write so many compositions, I had learned to research, take notes, make outlines, and condense large amounts of material into small spaces -- skills which are crucial to preparing assignments at undergraduate and graduate levels of work.

There is also the oral composition, which provides the pupil with an excellent introduction to public speaking. I always preferred oral compositions to written ones because they took much less time to complete. Mother helped me make notes on the subject of my choice, and after a little review, I stood and made my presentation to the class. I was never allowed to use my notes while speaking; I had to rely strictly upon my memory. Mother always evaluated my talk when I had finished, and her evaluation assisted me in improving those areas which needed work. At the time, I felt that oral compositions were a tremendous waste of effort -- though still preferable to written ones -- but when I attended seminars at BYU and was required to make presentations before students and faculty, I realized how valuable these years of practice had been.

Of course, proper grammar is critical to communicative writing, and several times a week the student is assigned a grammar lesson. In the eighth grade, grammar, vocabulary and composition are lumped together under one heading, and one of the three is assigned each day. Even in the earlier grades, vocabulary is stressed and the spelling books include a vocabulary lesson with each spelling lesson.

The Calvert course also stresses science, mathematics, and geography. Science is assigned several times a week starting in the third grade and continuing through the eighth. The books provide an elementary introduction to scientific terms and principles. In the seventh grade the text is devoted to elementary physics. While the science books used by Calvert do teach Darwinism, the school is very respectful of students' religious beliefs and allows parents to omit certain portions of science lessons -- including the entire eighth grade science course -- on the basis of religious objections.

Mathematics is assigned daily and includes the study of fractions, decimals, graphs, the Pythagorean theorem, and the metric system. In the seventh and eighth grades, simple geometry and algebra are included.

Geography includes both a study of U.S. and world geography. The child learns about the climate, landforms, and natural conditions of the area he is studying. He also learns about the populations, agriculture, and major industries of the area and is taught a little about the people and their customs. In the seventh grade geography is devoted entirely to a study of *Europe and the Soviet Union,* which provides the pupil with a greater understanding of and appreciation for the lifestyles of the people living in the Eastern Hemisphere. In the eighth grade geography is not assigned.

Such a program provides the student with a great deal of knowledge on a variety of subjects. Yet, as complete as the Calvert program is, Mother found ways to improve it. Shortly after our move into New Mexico, my parents purchased a twelve-foot long solid oak table and twelve oak chairs. The table was placed in a large room with one glass wall overlooking the backyard, and this room became both the dining room and our classroom. Every morning at 8:30 when the session began, each child was supposed to bring his manual to Mother. She looked over the daily lessons and assigned each of us a subject on which to begin working. We, then, took our places at the table -- Mother at the head, the youngest students on either side of her, and the older children a little further down. The children who could work independently did so, while Mother worked with one child on a difficult subject such as math. Later, she would assign that child a reading lesson which he could complete without supervision, while she helped another child.

Thus, she made good use of all her time, and saw to it that each child received the individual attention he required. If anyone had a question, he was to bring his books and work and stand behind Mother's chair until she was ready to assist him. On some harried days, I have seen as many as five children behind Mother's chair waiting for either an assignment or some assistance!

The process continued until 11:30 each morning and resumed again at 1:00 each afternoon. There are some people who use the terms "correspondence study" and "independent study" interchangeably. Independent study implies working independent of a teacher's direct and immediate supervision.

Personally, I prefer the term "correspondence study" since during the entire time I was in school I never worked completely independently. Far from it, I worked under the constant supervision of a most demanding and exacting tutor.

Yet, supervision did not mean that she ever did our work for us. There were often days when she thought that we were simply waiting for her to complete our assignments. On these occasions she would say, "Just do it the way you think it should be done, and when you are through I will check your work." She was willing to spend hours explaining areas which confused us, but when the time came for the actual work to be done, we had to do it ourselves. We were not even allowed to use any of the aids which other teachers might find perfectly acceptable and even necessary. For instance, during the entire time that I was in school, we never owned a computer. Many people asked my mother why, and her reply was always the same. "I think that children can become too dependent on visual aids. I want my children to understand and possess basic skills without having to depend upon a machine every time they have to solve a problem or write a paper." Although later, after I graduated, we did purchase a home computer, it is used only to prepare undergraduate and graduate essays, and is off limits to the grade school children.

This philosophy was also responsible for the ban on the calculator. Even in high school, when I had to solve algebra and geometry problems, I was not allowed to use a calculator, either in my daily lessons or on my tests. It was very important to her that I be able to work out each step on my own, without any mechanical assistance.

School was a central part of our lives during those years. Everything else took a back seat to the "Three R's." No one who has not been involved in home-schooling could ever understand the role which education can play in a person's life. For children who attend regular schools, school is an important part of their lives, but it is external. It is outside of their homes and outside of their families. When the child is at school, he is in the "school environment" and when he is at home he is away from that environment. For the home-schooled child, the "school environment" is the one in which he spends most of his time. School is internal -- inside of his home, inside of his family, inside of him. It creeps into every conversation. In my family, when we are not talking about what one of the children is doing in school, we are discussing something one of us has studied. We seldom have a conversation in which school does not come up at least once.

I cannot help but wonder how many teenagers think they would like to live with their teacher -- not a teacher of only one subject, but rather a teacher who is well versed in every subject he has ever studied. Such a child would always be conscious of his grammar, because he would know that if he made a mistake, his teacher would immediately correct him. She would always be right, of course, because she would have taught grammar for so many years that she would know "all the rules." He would never confess that he had forgotten some mathematical principle, because he would know that she would be sure to assign him a refresher course. When asked, "Do you remember when we studied?. . ." he would always nod affirmatively, so that he would not have to relearn the material to which she was referring.

On the other hand, if he ever needed help in spelling a word, she could almost certainly give the correct spelling off the top of her head. If he needed assistance in writing a report, he could turn to her and she would be able to suggest information which should be included, ensure correct grammar and spelling, and help him to edit and proofread the final copy. And if he ever had a math problem of any kind which he simply could not solve, he would know that help was only as far away as his mother.

In my family the one non-student who also benefits from Mother's years of accumulated knowledge is my father. Often he asks her help with wording and transitions for reports which he has to prepare, but he has found that she is capable of providing other types of assistance as well. Once, when he had only a short time to figure a particularly difficult mathematical problem for a project on which he was working, he called Mother at home and asked her for help. Within minutes she had written a complicated algebraic equation, solved the problem, and called him back with the correct answer!

True, school plays a very important part in our lives, but it does not play the only role. It is said that, "All work and no play makes Jack a dull boy," and since my parents did not wish any of us to grow up to be dull, they made certain that we found time for the pleasant, restful moments with family which are at the core of a happy, well-balanced childhood.

Many of the happiest of these moments would not have been possible had we not been home-schooled. For example, about once a month a close friend of my mother's called her and told her to hurry and finish our lessons. On these afternoons, Mother let us out of school around two o'clock, and then she and her friend took all of us to Swensen's Ice-Cream Parlor for sundaes where we sat amid warm conversation and laughter while enjoying great frozen scoops of vanilla ice-cream draped with hot fudge sauce and whipped cream. We relished our treat, knowing that when we finished we had only to go home, eat another meal, and spend the evening with our father. We were blissfully ignorant of the fact that on these bleak winter afternoons less fortunate children all over the city were trudging back to their houses and an evening filled with homework. Later, Jan moved away, but recently I received a birthday card from her with a picture of an ice-cream sundae on the front and a note inside reading, "Dear Alexandra: Remember the ice-cream sundaes?" Instantly, I felt as though I had been transported back in time to the old-fashioned ice-cream parlor and the wonderful times we shared there.

Home-schooling made possible other special moments as well. Although I spent most of my time with my mother, because of my flexible schedule I also was able to spend a great deal of time with my father. Dad was the President-CEO of a large financial institution, and about once every two or three months he took me to his office and let me spend the day with him. Mother set my hair in curlers the night before, and that morning she carefully brushed and arranged it for me. I was then dressed, and I went off to the office with Daddy. Driving there we had long, soulful talks, as we discussed every aspect of my school work and I told him all the things which had been on my mind. He responded to my chatter by laughing and commenting as though I had been a miniature adult rather than a seven or eight-year-old child.

Then, all too quickly, we arrived at the building, and I was taken inside and introduced to some of his employees and members of the board of directors. At last my father, who had to begin work, took me into his office, closed the door, and commissioned me to entertain myself quietly until he could take me to lunch. All morning I watched him, as he hurried in and out of his office, sometimes entering only for a moment to make a telephone call. Usually some employee was on his heels asking a question, or a client might catch him and spend an hour or two talking to him about business. Even then I marveled at how busy he was, as I sat scribbling on a sheet of paper and dreaming of the day when school would be behind me and I, too, could work in an office such as his.

At twelve o'clock, he took a break for lunch, and he and I went to some restaurant and dined together. Usually, we went to the El Paso Club -- by far the most exclusive private club in El Paso. There, in the elegant atmosphere, with my father at my side, I felt like a princess. We were seated at a table by a window, where I could look down eighteen stories upon the city of El Paso as a tuxedoed waiter took my order for a lobster tail and a Coca Cola, and for dessert -- chocolate mousse. The meal and the conversation were always pleasant -- Dad seemed very interested in everything I said and did, and no matter how busy or preoccupied he might be, he was never too busy to listen to me. Sometimes he even discussed aspects of his work with me, as though I were old enough to understand the intricacies of finance, and I tried to respond as though I understood perfectly. Finally, it was time to leave, and we returned to the office, he to his work, and I to my play until at five o'clock he took me home tired but still bright-eyed from the excitement of the day.

Occasionally, I had the pleasure of being escorted out by both my parents -- just the three of us. This happened more often at my birthday than any other time. We agreed on a restaurant where I wanted to eat, and at the prescribed time Mother and I arrived at my father's office. All of us then went to lunch together, and we spent about an hour and a half eating, laughing, and talking. Afterwards, Mother took me to buy my birthday present.

The one other time when I had the opportunity to go out alone with my parents was when I finished a grade. They had a policy that as each child finished a grade in school they took the child to the restaurant of his or her choice. Some of these outings were very special. For instance, when I finished the eighth grade, my parents took me to a local dinner theater to see a production of *Bye Bye Birdie*. During dinner, my parents told me how proud they were of me, and how confident they were that I would perform beautifully in high school. Then my father gave me two lovely gold necklaces and my mother gave me a gold ring studded with sapphires which I had admired since the day I first spotted it in her jewelry box. I thought how blessed I must be to have two such loving, wonderful parents. Though the food was not impressive, nor the performance spectacular, the atmosphere that night was very festive, and the evening stands out as one of the happiest of my life.

These moments were the closest I ever came to knowing what it must be like to be an only child. Yet, someone once remarked that my parents were the only people she knew who had ten "only" children, and I believe that there is considerable truth in this statement. This may be due partially to the fact that we were always home-schooled. While my parents would have been doting even if they had sent us to more conventional schools, it is a fact that home-schooling forces a parent to view each child as an individual. The parent must separate each child from the rest of the group and evaluate his or her strengths and weaknesses. Perhaps this one-on-one approach makes possible a more personal relationship with each child. In any case, every child in our family always received completely equal treatment with every other child, and all of us spent a great deal of time with each of our parents.

In addition to these times spent individually with our parents, we spent much time together as a family. Holidays are always festive occasions in our home. Thanksgiving is often the holiday when we invite guests. Mother and my sisters and I are up early that morning, preparing the turkey for roasting, and baking pies. The pies are always the same -- pumpkin and pecan, with lots of fresh whipped cream. The rest of the meal -- a fruit salad, cornbread dressing, mashed potatoes with gravy, homemade noodles, and homemade cranberry sauce -- takes several hours to prepare, for Mother always makes everything from scratch. Before the company arrives, she sets the long oak dining table with silver and fine china, while my father lays a huge fire in the fireplace. Then, when the guests arrive and we are ready to eat, another Swann tradition comes into play -- before beginning, my father says a blessing and then one at a time, each person tells one event which has happened to him during the past year for which he is thankful. Later that evening, when the guests are gone, we finish our day by taking a long walk together in the chilly autumn twilight.

Christmas is a holiday generally set apart for the family, but one which we celebrate for nearly the entire month of December. As early as December 10, Mother purchases a Christmas tree. An evening or two later we hold a tree-decorating party. Between sips of eggnog and mouthfuls of chocolate fudge, children run back and forth, from tree to ornaments, joyously dangling brightly colored balls. In theory, the older children help the younger ones, but usually the smaller children are left to themselves and hang their decorations in spots they can easily reach rather than in places where the ornaments would look best. Finally, at eight o'clock the bedlam dies, order is restored, and all children under ten years old are sent to bed. Mother then inspects the tree and usually finds a clump of balls in one spot, while other places are virtually bare. It is then her duty to redistribute the decorations in an attractive manner.

With the tree in place, we spend every evening for about two weeks wrapping Christmas gifts and placing them under the tree, until by Christmas Eve the room more resembles a department store than a private residence. By then, however, our labors are finished, for "Twas the night before Christmas and all through the house," another celebration is taking place. Rather than preparing a regular dinner that evening we set out a buffet of treats -- olive cheese ball with crackers, fudge, the five-pound box of Russell Stovers candy from my grandmother, nut bread, fruitcake, assorted chips and dips, chicken liver paté, homemade nachos, and soft drinks. After "dinner" we unwrap our presents and then spend a quiet evening watching television together. The following day we continue the festivities with a large holiday meal. For many years the celebration included Mother having her newest reader in school read to the family "The Christmas Story," a version of the enunciation and birth of Christ written on a first grade level. A joyful, festive spirit always prevails during these holidays which makes it impossible for any of us not to feel contented just to be with one another.

By Christmas night, we are tired and almost glad that the following day we will resume our normal schedule. At this point, my father carries out a rather unusual tradition of his own -- "the torching of the tree." Dad hates to have the tree up after Christmas, so when the festivities have ended on Christmas night, he has us take all the ornaments off the tree and pack them away. He then cuts the tree into small pieces and burns it in the fireplace. Thus, we end our holiday by sending the Christmas tree up in smoke!

Time in such an idyllic environment passes more quickly than anyone would hope. Almost before we were aware of what was happening, I had finished all eight grades at Calvert and was ready to progress on to a secondary school. By this time I was ten years old, and Mother had been tutoring me a little over five years. In spite of my unusually young age, I had never skipped a grade or even a day's lesson. As far as my parents were concerned, the speed with which I was completing my studies was merely a pleasant side effect of home-schooling; it certainly was not the most important factor. What really mattered was that I was receiving the best possible education, and to my parents this involved attending and mastering each grade level, with no omissions. Because of this attitude, they would not have considered allowing me to skip all or any part of my high school studies, for they felt that grades 9-12 constituted an essential part of my education.

However, they wanted Mother to continue as my tutor, and this involved enrolling me in an accredited correspondence high school. We were not at all certain that we could even find such a school. In fact, many of my parents' friends assured them that the very idea was ludicrous. The feeling of deja vu must have been incredible; once again Mother and Dad were being told that their goals were impossible. "No one has ever attended high school at home, and no one ever will," they were told. Even if by some fluke they were able to locate a correspondence high school, how would Mother tutor me through subjects such as algebra and geometry, which she had not studied for many years? Where would she find the time?

Nearly every year brought us either a new baby or a new student, or both. In July of 1979 Dominic began school, and in September of the same year, Israel was born. On Christmas Day 1980, our eighth child, Gabrielle was born, and the following March Victoria began school. Mother now had eight children, five of whom she was teaching. She could not possibly have the time or the energy to take on the exhausting responsibility of teaching high school.

Besides, claimed the skeptics, even if all of the above were possible, how could my father continue to pay for these expensive private schools? He was already funding private educations for five children in addition to supporting his large family. How long could our situation be expected to last?

As Fate would have it, our situation was to outlast the skeptics. Mother and Dad were far more optimistic about the prospect of my entering high school -- after all, she had already proven these same people wrong about her ability to tutor me through elementary school. I had completed my studies at an accelerated rate, and had made excellent grades in the process. Mother had finished high school, and she felt that with a comprehensive program she should have no difficulty tutoring me through this area of study. Dad also felt that she would be successful. Whatever the rest of the world might say, he never doubted for a minute that their plan would work perfectly nor that it was worth every cent that it cost him. Together, they decided to begin trying to locate a program.

Finding such a program might present some difficulty since nearly "everyone" was convinced that no such institution existed. However, my father contacted Harry Marcoplis, who at that time was the Headmaster of Calvert School, and asked if he could recommend a suitable high school. Marcoplis advised my father to contact the American School in Chicago, Illinois, stating that the school has a program through which a student can earn a high school diploma entirely through correspondence -- the four year program is thoroughly accredited, providing the pupil with a nationally recognized diploma. My parents were very interested, and they promptly contacted the school about enrolling me.

The American School was hesitant to enroll me for two reasons. First, they wanted to make certain that we were acting in full compliance with state law. However, with Papen's, Noland's, and Johnson's letters in our possession, we were easily able to prove that this was the case. In addition, Charles Noland also wrote a letter to Mary Mckeown, principal of the American School, explaining New Mexico's laws regarding education, and confirming that we were in full compliance, so this matter was quickly resolved. The second and more significant reason for their hesitation was that they feared I would be incapable of performing at a high school level. The American School program has been designed for adults who have never earned a high school diploma, and although my grades at Calvert had been impressive, school officials felt that a ten-year-old simply would not possess the emotional and intellectual maturity to master the curriculum. However, they did agree to accept me on an experimental basis.

The American School is designed so that sixteen units are necessary for graduation if the student is enrolled in the college preparatory program. The program was broken down into eleven required units and five elective units. The required units comprised the following courses:'

Understanding English I	1 unit
Understanding English II	1 unit
American Literature	1 unit
English Literature	1 unit
Biology (lab or non lab)	1 unit
Psychology	1 unit
United States History	1 unit
Social Civics (Government)	1 unit
Essential Mathematics I	1 unit
Algebra I	1 unit
Plane Geometry	1 unit

The choices for electives ranged from language and art courses to courses in business and automotive design.

Immediately, Mother took the lead in selecting my electives. She could see that my first choices would have been subjects I thought would be less challenging, such as courses in home economics, and child care. Therefore, she insisted that I enroll in more scholarly courses, such as English, speech, and world literature. My father, after personally reviewing all of my choices for electives, decided that it was important for me to take at least one course in business, and enrolled me in accounting. I was allowed to choose one course, and I selected "shorthand." Thus, my curriculum was established.

I finished the eighth grade with Calvert in July of 1980, but it was September before my first course arrived from the American School. The two and a half month hiatus was the longest I had ever experienced. Mother had kept me busy doing simple household chores and assisting her with the other children's lessons. Although I had enjoyed my break, I was delighted when my materials arrived and I could begin to do some work for myself again.

I found that my first course, Psychology for Life Today was totally unlike anything I had studied in Calvert. The book came with a manual containing instructions, assignments, and written tests. Each morning Mother previewed my day's lesson with me, explaining anything which I did not understand. I then completed the lesson, and the self-check test based on the material which I had studied that day. Afterwards, Mother checked my answers against those which were included in the manual, and she and I discussed whatever mistakes I had made. After every three or four lessons, I completed a test which was mailed to the school. Because these tests were based on comprehension rather than memory, the manual advised me to use my textbooks to complete the tests. This obviously made test taking considerably more pleasant and less harried.

After I had been enrolled for a few months, the courses began arriving in groups of two's and three's. Mother had me working on one subject, such as algebra, in the morning and a different subject, such as English, in the afternoon. This alternation of courses not only accelerated the rate of my progress, it gave me some relief from the monotony of concentrating on only one subject. Calvert had prepared me so well that I was already familiar with much of the material, and this also accelerated my progress. Even in the literature courses, I recognized many of the authors and their work, and this greatly reduced the amount of time and effort which had to be expended on my schoolwork. However, my greatest asset was, as usual, my tutor.

When Mother testified at *Leeper vs. Arlington*, one of the principal objections being raised by the assistant attorney general against home-schooling was that in the course of attempting to teach the child, a parent may encounter subjects which he or she has not studied for many years or has never studied. At that point, the home-schooler will be unable to continue tutoring and will be forced to place the child in school.

When questioned on this subject, Mother replied, "Well, you must understand that there is one requirement for the home-schooling parent -- he must be at least as smart as his student. If he is at least as smart as his student, he will have no difficulty whatsoever, and if he is just a little smarter, he will have a distinct advantage."

Mother is easily a little smarter than any of her students, and she further increased her advantage by reading every book assigned to me and reviewing every assignment. It was a policy she had begun in Calvert, but in the American School it became especially important and time consuming. She spent many evenings, after a long day of teaching school, reading lengthy books. She tried to make certain that she was ahead of me so that if I had any questions about my work, she would be familiar with the material.

When the time came for me to begin algebra and geometry, her evenings were spent solving all of the problems in the following day's lesson so that she could teach me how to solve them. As she studied these texts, she found ways to simplify lengthy procedures, eliminate confusing steps and, in short, reduce algebra and geometry to their simplest terms. These evening study sessions were neither pleasant nor relaxing for her, but they proved highly productive, for during these hours she developed significant teaching techniques which were of great help to her in leading me through the complicated maze of high school mathematics. I was not involved in these evening study sessions -- I saw only the results of her labors each day in class as she systematically taught each subject.

Mother encouraged me to work independently as much as possible. I worked the problems without help and then checked my answers against those in the book. Yet, she also scheduled time nearly every day for us to work together. Whenever I missed a problem, she would sit down with me and determine where I had made the mistake. Because she had worked the problems the night before, it was a simple matter for her to find my error and show me how to correct it. Although she had as many as five students during the time that I was in high school, she always found time to give each of us individual instruction.

This, in my opinion, is one of the great benefits of being educated at home. When children attend public or private schools, they are part of a class, and the class often dictates the level of learning. At home, however, the instruction is customized to suit the individual needs of each child. Thus, each child constitutes a class where his personal educational needs are met. No matter how many classes the home-schooling mother may have, each class contains only one student. As a result, each child is able to reach his fullest potential without being limited by the abilities of those around him. In my case, this one-on-one interaction -- which I could not have hoped to receive in a regular classroom -- was critical to my mastering high school material.

The entire four-year program, with books and instruction manuals, cost only five hundred dollars at the time I enrolled. In addition, the school works out a monthly payment schedule appropriate to the student's budget. While it may seem extravagant to pay for a private high school, when one considers the cost of clothing, lunches, and transportation for four years of public high school, five hundred dollars is really not expensive.

Of course, there were some things that the five hundred dollars tuition could not buy. At my high school, there was no prom, no senior trip, no boys, no female friends with whom to chat on the telephone, and no graduation day. I can honestly say that I did not miss any of these in the least. In the first place, I always had my family close by, and they compensated for any social contacts I might have missed. In the second place, I have always disliked ceremony, as is proven by the fact that when I graduated from college, I chose not to attend the commencement ceremonies at Brigham Young University. Thus, I never felt deprived because I did not have a high school graduation ceremony.

Because of my unusually young age, I feel that had I attended a regular high school, the results might have been disastrous. A ten-year-old would most certainly be treated as a misfit and scorned as a "baby" by his older classmates. Besides, I had always been home-schooled, and therefore, it seemed only natural that I would attend high school at home. Although I was aware that my situation was different from that of other young people, I really could not imagine any other way of life.

Finally, there was another major factor separating me from most other high schoolers -- the speed with which I earned my diploma. Within eighteen months from the time I enrolled, I had completed the four-year program at the American School. I had managed to attend twelve grades without ever leaving the comfort and security of my home. My next area of study remained undecided.

THREE
THE BENEVOLENT TYRANTS

Presiding over this complicated routine are my mother and father -- "the benevolent tyrants." Actually, the appellation is thoroughly appropriate, for the word "tyrant" originates from a Greek word meaning "one who rules with absolute power." Yet, though they reign as dictators, their tyranny is always of a benevolent nature. Their combination of a firm but gentle rule over their home is a major factor in our family's accomplishments.

Few children are blessed with two more talented parents. My father, who has worked in finance for over twenty years, is now an independent financial consultant specializing in banking institutions. In 1980 he received a Doctor of Humane Letters Degree from Linda Vista Baptist Bible College and Seminary. He has appeared in *Who's Who in the South and Southwest, Who's Who in Finance and Industry, The International Who's Who of Intellectuals,* and *Personalities of the South.*

Mother, who now has more than thirteen years of teaching experience to her credit, was awarded Eagle Forum's "Full Time Homemaker of the Year Award" for the state of New Mexico in 1985. In addition, she has twice been summoned as an expert witness in court cases deciding whether home-schooling should be legalized. In *Leeper vs. Arlington,* the first of these cases, the judge expressed special appreciation for her testimony, and later ruled in the home-schoolers' favor. Where her own teaching program is concerned, she has taught every grade from first through a master's program -- and as many as fifty-four subjects simultaneously. Her students include the three youngest graduates in the history of Brigham Young University.

In 1988 my parents celebrated their twenty-fifth wedding anniversary -- a quarter of a century spent together in the ultimate partnership. Though twenty-five years ago when John Swann and Joyce Degele were married they probably envisioned someday celebrating their silver wedding anniversary, they could not possibly have known the unusual course their lives would take.

The last twenty-five years have not all been easy ones -- there have been bitter disappointments and setbacks along with the triumphs. Yet, through all of their difficulties their love and understanding for one another has always remained strong, and they have passed that strength on to their children. From them we have learned that the secret to a successful life is not in what one receives, but in how one deals with what is given to him. No life can be entirely free from pain, but my parents have tried to teach each of us to bear life's hardships well while always demanding the best of ourselves.

The lessons they have taught us extend far beyond those learned in any classroom -- even one at home. They have instilled in us the values of perseverance, industry, a sense of responsibility, a healthy respect for others, and a strong sense of right and wrong. Much of this we have learned through their example, for my parents practice what they preach. They have been protective and supportive, cheering us on in our moments of success, encouraging us in our moments of failure, and defending us against critics.

Our lives have centered around their philosophy that anything can be accomplished through prayer and old-fashioned hard work. In the office Dad poured himself into his job, while at home Mother organized her day to complete her many domestic tasks. For several years, Mother rose at five-thirty each morning to begin her household duties. When we were old enough to help, she assigned us jobs around the house also. Then everyone rose at six o'clock and began his tasks. Francesca and I set the breakfast table, Victoria washed the breakfast dishes, Christopher and Dominic fed the dog and cleaned the yard. I vacuumed the carpets daily and Francesca cleaned all the bathrooms. Mother personally took care of all the laundry -- we usually had between four and five loads a day -- and she and I swept and mopped all the hard surface floors. Much of this work was done before school began at eight-thirty.

Everyone was expected to do his part without complaint, knowing that all of us worked together. The result was that in spite of the fact that there were ten children and Mother taught all of us, she still managed to keep a clean house.

She was equally determined that her other maternal duties would not be neglected. I used to laugh because Mother talked to even newborns as though they were much older children. For years she held and breastfed her babies while teaching school. As the children grew a little older, she continued to spend time with them after class, talking to them, playing games with them, and sometimes just sitting and watching television while holding them. During school hours she did not allow them to interrupt, but she tried to find ways for them to occupy themselves. Often she allowed them to color quietly with crayons, or play with toys in another room.

Her dedication was perhaps most evident in the classroom, however. Mother forced herself to think of her schooling not in terms of a hobby or an activity, but in terms of a vocation. The word vocation actually comes from the Latin word, "vocare," which means "to call." Mother feels that home-schooling is truly a calling, and that it deserves her best effort. Consequently, she has worked to improve her own teaching techniques so that she may better educate her children. Without assistance, she invented a device which makes it possible to clearly and effectively teach metrics to even a small child. Her phonics system can teach a five-year-old with no previous reading readiness to read within six weeks. She has invented a means of teaching positive and negative integers, and has simplified high school algebra and geometry by discovering ways to eliminate many confusing steps. She has even discovered an amazingly simple means for memorizing the circle of fifths -- a musical device listing sharps and flats of all notes. Professional teachers have asked for some of these techniques, because they are both simple and effective.

Juggling so many responsibilities could be very taxing, but fortunately, Mother has enormous will power. She is not "superwoman," but she does appear to have an abundance of energy and she seldom becomes overly tired. Once in a while in a fit of frustration she used to shake her head and say that she was considering taking all of us out of her program and sending us to public school because she simply felt overwhelmed and did not believe that she could go on teaching us any longer. I grew very upset when she would say such things, for I half expected her to go through with it. I later realized that the statement was a veiled but effective threat -- it never failed to encourage us to speed up our efforts. In reality I can imagine no circumstances under which she would have refused to tutor us.

Even now she never expresses a desire for a more relaxed life. On the contrary, she sometimes amuses me because she prides herself on being able to do two things at once. "I am a person," she admits, "who finds it almost impossible to sit still for more than a few minutes unless sitting still is a necessary part of some project such as teaching." Sometimes it seems that she is overextending herself, and that it would be better for her not to take on so much at one time. Yet, Mother seems very content. "It has been my experience that people put too much emphasis on having time for themselves," she says. "I find that I am far healthier and far happier than women my age who have pursued careers, scheduled 'quiet time' for themselves to be alone and meditate, and been careful not to 'overextend' themselves."

Though she devotes very little time to herself, Mother does have a life beyond acting as mother and teacher to her children. She exercises daily with the family's "home gym" and when the weather is pleasant, she and my father try to walk four miles a day. She is an excellent cook, and prepares wonderful meals for the family, but she, herself, diets frequently, and actually eats less than any individual I have ever known. She exists almost solely on raw fruit in summer, and raw vegetables in winter. Some of her concoctions have been less than appetizing -- Christopher titled one particularly unsavory looking mixture "MedEVIL Soup" -- but she sticks to her diets without complaint in an attempt to keep her figure (an attempt which has met with such good results that many people comment that they would never even suspect she has had ten children.)

Most importantly, however, she is able to keep her sense of humor. Home-schooling is an exhausting, time consuming, often frustrating endeavor, and it is my opinion that the really successful home-schooler must be able to have a good laugh every now and then. Mother never takes herself or the world around her too seriously, and she is able to spread a little humor to us when life begins to get difficult. In her few spare moments she enjoys writing, and though her works include short stories and serious poetry, she prefers to write humorous poetry about the more frustrating aspects of everyday life. Her subject matter includes everything from dieting, to old age, to motherhood. Because her works are as unique as they are genuinely funny, I have included a few so that my readers may have a small glimpse of the lighter side of Joyce Swann:

The Diet

Mary Beth Mahoney
Had grown a little fat,
Of all her clothes
The only thing that fit her was her hat.

Mary Beth was saddened
That she'd come to such a state,
She drew herself to her full height
And vowed, "I will lose weight."

She hurried to the bookstore
To seek some sage advice,
And purchased every diet book
Whose title sounded "nice."

The ice-cream diet ordered
That she eat three times a day,
Great frozen scoops of ice-cream
To melt the pounds away.

One fed her carbohydrates,
One this, another that,
A fourth said, "Only alcohol
Can burn away that fat!"

She was never so bewildered
As she'd been about those diets,
She really must decide on one
And make herself apply it.

Then from deep within her brain
Came the answer like a bolt,
It exploded in her head,
Oh, it gave her quite a jolt!

The answer was so simple
She knew that she must try it,
She'd pack advice from each of them
Into one colossal diet!

She worked with fevered passion,
To stock each pantry shelf
With alcoholic beverages
And bread she baked herself.

The fats and carbohydrate foods
She stacked up to the ceiling,
As she thought of all the weight she'd lose
With such a happy feeling.

She'd never had a drink before
(It was just a little quirk)
But she knew she'd have to "bottoms up"
To make this diet work.

Morning, noon and night,
She ate and drank her fill,
Guzzling and gorging,
She displayed an iron will.

Yes, Mary Beth succeeded,
For she found the ideal diet,
It is the "perfect way of eating,"
Surely no one can deny it.

Well, Mary Beth's now happy
But the gossips in our town,
Say she's become a drunken bum
And weighs three hundred pounds.

The Impostor

There's a woman in my mirror
Who's impersonating me,
Though I really can't imagine
Who the hag might be.

She looks a little like me
Around her mouth and nose,
She's copied all my hairstyles,
And dresses in my clothes.

As I've grown a little older,
And middle age approaches,
She's sprouted crow's feet deep as ruts
And bags as big as brooches.

She uses all my beauty aids,
I've seen her with my potions,
She lavishes on my night creams
And revels in my lotions.

Her hair is getting gray
And her jaw is loose and slack,
But if you think she looks bad from the front,
You should view her from the back.

Her hips have gone all saggy,
They hang down like a bag,
How did she get inside my mirror?
This unrelenting hag.

The straw that broke the camel's back,
Was when I woke today
To find her peering from my mirror,
Her hair in wild array.

The sight was simply awful,
It nearly stopped my heart,
And I made my mind up then and there --
Our company must part.

I looked her squarely in the eye,
But all that I could say,
Was, "I don't know how you got here,
But please, please go away!"

Finally, she wrote the following rhyme several years prior to being nominated "Full Time Homemaker of the Year":

Credentials

The ladies of our town once chose
To have my name appear
Upon a list of candidates,
For "Mother of the Year."

The day soon came when, in my turn,
Before the board I went
To pale before the scrutiny
Of Madam President.

Here it comes! I feel it coming!
The idiotic question,
Delivered with a simpering smile,
Pregnant with suggestion.

With crinkled eyes and out-thrust chin,
And lips set in a smirk.
In oily tones she makes the query,
"I wonder, do you work?"

"I rise at five, retire at twelve,"
I reply, in turn,
"I wash and cook and scrub and sew,
I bake my bread and churn."

"No, no," she coos with evil glee,
"That is not what I meant,
The thing by which you must be judged
is some *accomplishment.*"

"My children never went to school,
I taught them all myself,
And they have trophies two abreast
On every household shelf."

She shakes her head and clucks her tongue,
Her face grows black with scorn,
I see that I must surely be
A civic leader's thorn.

Question after question
She fires with deadly force,
But back I come time after time
To those silly kids, of course.

When the grilling ceases,
I sit alone and wait,
To ponder all my blunders
As the committee deliberates.

If virtue is its own reward,
I reason on this day,
Then Motherhood must also be
Its own best resume.

I hear at last approaching steps,
My ear is quickly bent
To hear the clicking of the heels
Of Madam President.

She thus approaches with disdain,
Her face is cold and grim,
Her glassy eyes look into mine,
My hopes are growing slim.

"We've agreed upon a candidate,
Though she's childless,
You'll agree she is a paragon
Of what a Mother *ought* to be.

Thank you for appearing,
But I do greatly fear
That Motherhood is *not* enough
For 'Mother of the Year.' "

The ability to find a humorous side in most situations is a trait
which both my parents share. "Most of the time in this life you
can either laugh or cry," Dad once told me. "I prefer to laugh."
In our house, laughter really is the best medicine.

42

As the head of the household, Dad has been very instrumental in our upbringings. Although he does not participate in the teaching of scholastics, like all loving fathers, he has taught us other important lessons. One of the greatest of these has been in the virtue of tenacity. Dad believes that nothing is impossible, and therefore, he never takes "no" for an answer. Once the financial institution where he served as President-CEO was undergoing a major expansion because of a merger with an offshore facility. Dad was working feverishly to have necessary phone and computer lines installed between the two institutions in order to facilitate business transactions. In the course of one conversation with AT&T regarding this matter, he stated that he wanted the computers "on line" immediately. The representative from AT&T responded that this was impossible -- it would be more than a month before the necessary lines could be installed. "A month!" snapped my father, "you should be able to conquer the world in a month!" The lines were installed considerably under the month deadline.

Many of the moments we have shared with my father have been happy and colorful. Once when we were small he and Mother took all of us to an Italian restaurant for dinner. They allowed us to order whatever we liked, and we feasted on an enormous meal of pizza, spaghetti, chicken Jerusalem, ravioli, and for dessert, cheesecake. As we prepared to leave the restaurant, the cashier gave us each a lollipop. One of the small children, noticing his flavor, complained, "I don't like this one. I want strawberry."

"Be quiet," my father ordered, "There's no such thing as strawberry!"

Although maintaining our unusual lifestyle has often required sacrifices on his part, Dad is fiercely proud of his family and feels that it is one which would be "envied and coveted" by many people. He has always worked to teach his children to appreciate our homelife and to be grateful that we have a loving family.

"My parents used to pick out one member of the family to harass and the other members of the family would gang up on them," he often tells us. "In this family, we don't do that. We don't criticize one another, and we are not petty about each other. When one member succeeds, we are all happy for that person. We support each other's ideas -- even if we do not think they will work. No member of this family has ever said to any other member, 'I did something for you and so you owe me.' "

"Some parents take the attitude that if their children want

an education beyond the twelfth grade, they will have to get out and earn at least part of the money themselves. We haven't taken that approach with you. We don't ever say, 'I put you through a master's degree program, so you, are going to have to pay me back someday, because, frankly, we don't want anything in return. In today's modern nuclear family, this type of love and support is very rare."

However, Dad believes that discipline is essential to a tranquil family life. We have always had a great deal of discipline in our home, which has led to a rare combination of order and serenity in our household. Each of us, including my mother, recognizes and respects my father as the head of the household, and my mother as the head when he is not present. Their word is law. "I believe that strict discipline is imperative, or I would not be the person I am today," says Dad, adding that a lack of discipline can be very costly, particularly when it leads to problems such as drug and alcohol use. "People get arrested, and they have to put up money for bail, or they have accidents and have to be hospitalized. Also, the cost of supporting a drug habit and the cost of rehabilitation can be financially devastating. Aside from a purely financial aspect, however, an undisciplined child can be an emotional burden as well. I am a person who simply could not have coped with having a child on drugs," he states, adding, "I believe that the greatest bonus of strict discipline is freedom from worry -- which is priceless."

Although he has been strict with us, my father feels that this has been good for us. "i feel that children are abandoned to the world much too young. They get into terrible trouble, not because they mean to, but because they don't know better. They are young, innocent and native, but they don't stay that way for long. It's really very sad."

"Of all the pecan trees which have grown up in our back yard, which one grew the best?" He pauses, looking thoughtfully at me, and then continues, "The one which grew up in the shade of another tree. It was the tallest and the healthiest, and so far the only one that we have been able to transplant. The larger tree protected it from the wind and sheltered it from the heat. Even the hot sun can scorch a tender shoot. That is really what children are -- tender shoots. If they are raised in a loving, protective environment, they grow strong like that little tree, and when they go out into the world, they are not nearly so vulnerable."

Both of my parents are incredibly protective, but Dad has always been a primary source of both discipline and support in our home and Mother feels that in these two ways he has been central to our program. "John is the most remarkable man I know -- a rare treasure who is undoubtedly largely responsible for the success of our program," she says of my father. "Although he has never been a part of the teaching process, without him this program would not have worked. Perhaps the most important role that John has played in our home-schooling program has been in the area of his unreserved support. He encouraged me when I felt frightened and inadequate. He always believed in me, and he helped me to believe in myself."

Another area in which Dad has been essential to the program's success is that of financial support. Though he shrugs this contribution off by saying that he never really thought about the expense because for many years he made a good salary, Mother is more vocal about the price Dad has paid. "Instead of buying a new car, he pays for master's degree programs. Instead of going on a well-deserved vacation, he writes out a check for more tuitions. Yet, with all his sacrifices he has never hesitated. When he speaks about finances it is not in terms of what he wants for himself; rather, he says how grateful he is that we have been able to keep all of our children on this accelerated program of study."

Mother believes that having been home-schooled will be a great asset to us in our adult lives. "Each of my children seems to think that there is nothing he cannot do and do very well. I think home-schooling has made them very individualistic, very independent and very confident. Because of these qualities, I expect them to do well in whatever careers they may choose," she says.

My father believes that because we have been home-schooled, we will probably have a great deal of self-confidence. He expects that we will not be afraid to compete with others for jobs because we will feel that we have the background and ability to succeed at whatever we attempt. He also believes that as a result of having been home-schooled we may be much more independent and self-reliant than we might otherwise have been and that, as a result, some of us may start our own businesses and work for ourselves. However, he does not believe that monetary gain will ever be the primary focus of our efforts. He feels that we will probably prove to be excellent employees because we will take pride in our work and do the best possible job. "Because you have been taught that 'second is nothing' you will attempt to be the best," he tells me.

Perhaps the only area in which Mother and Dad do not totally agree is in the rate of speed at which such a program should be completed. Mother is very firm on this point. "I see so many teens and pre-teens who are bored. They have so much time with nothing to do when they are growing up; they might as well be doing something constructive. Look at all the young women who are trying to get degrees and work at the same time; maybe they have a baby, too. They're wearing themselves out."

Dad takes a slightly different approach. "One of the things that concerned me was the rate at which the children were progressing through school. They were maturing academically much faster than they were maturing emotionally. I was not afraid that they could not do the work, because I knew they could, but I did worry about what would happen when they had their master's degrees at sixteen. At sixteen if you want to work you have to go to the local McDonalds. I think that it would be very bad emotionally for a sixteen-year-old with a master's degree to end up working for minimum wage. At eighteen or nineteen, you can go out into the work force with a master's degree and people can accept it better. We (Joyce and I) had several talks about that, but I never won."

Mother shakes her head, "It's better to get your education out of the way when you're young," she says. "It simplifies the rest of your life."

FOUR
A CHANGE OF SEASONS

September of 1982 had arrived and summer prepared to surrender her golden throne to frosty autumn. At first, the changes were hardly noticeable -- the grass remained green and the trees were still thick with their emerald leaves. The desert plants gave no sign that they would soon be falling into a deep sleep. Yet, a tinge of fall was undeniably present, and it manifested itself in a hundred small ways -- the days began to grow slightly cooler and shorter while the evening shadows grew a little longer.

I, too, was undergoing changes, and though they seemed small and insignificant, they signaled the undeniable fact that I would soon be leaving childhood behind. My physical appearance was changing -- I had begun to experience the trauma of braces and eyeglasses. The eyeglasses had by now given way to contact lenses, but I would have to live with braces until I was thirteen. My clothing and shoe sizes had been permanently established. I was even being allowed to dabble into a little makeup -- I could now wear very pale lipglosses and nail polishes.

Intellectually I was also maturing, though the process was naturally slower. I was beginning to take an interest in the artistic and creative. Perhaps the first manifestation of this new bent lay in my establishment of a Christmas play. For several years each fall I selected a play, conducted rehearsals and then directed the younger children in a performance for Mother and Dad on Christmas Eve. The play, unfortunately, met with strong resistance from my brothers and sisters, who had been begged, blackmailed, or bribed into assuming their roles. Although I personally derived hours of pleasure from the enterprise, after a few years the complaints became so vocal and the complainers so staunch in their protests that the Christmas play finally died a natural death.

Another favorite pastime was reading. I had always read a great deal of extra-curricular material, but during the years between eleven and fourteen I widened my literary horizons. I filled my hours with such classics as *Quo Vadis, The Last Days of Pompeii, A Tale of Two Cities,* and *The Robe,* as well as a number of excellent non-fiction works.

Our family was also growing and changing. Christopher was now ten and in high school -- he would be turning eleven in two months. In another year he should be graduating, but he was moving so fast that I feared he might finish before then, thus beating the record I had set. Francesca, nine, was in the eighth grade and would soon begin high school. Dominic, eight, was in the seventh grade, Victoria, six, was in the fourth grade and Benjamin, four, would be starting school in nine months. My parents' ninth child, Stefan, had been born on September 1. They were very busy caring for all of their babies and teaching their older children.

Only one year before, my brother Israel, who was then two, had spent three weeks in the hospital undergoing a series of major surgeries to remove an intestinal blockage. A similar surgery had been performed when he was fourteen months old, and his current illness was due to an adhesion which had formed because of the handling of the bowel. The adhesion had wrapped itself around his intestine, cutting off all circulation and necessitating surgery. Because the doctors misdiagnosed his condition, by the time that the operation was performed, gangrene had set in. My brother, who is *not* diabetic, had gone into diabetic shock. Eight inches of his intestine had to be removed, and for three weeks he lay at death's door, while Mother and Dad took shifts staying with him at the hospital.

Although my parents did not want him to be alone at the hospital for even one moment, they also felt that my brothers and sisters and I were too young to stay alone all day. Therefore, they arranged for friends to stay with us during the day while Mother stayed with Israel and Dad worked. After work my father came home to bathe and change. He then drove to the hospital, usually arriving between nine and ten o'clock at night to relieve my mother, who had been there since eight o'clock that morning. When she got home, she ate a sandwich while starting the laundry, for although friends were staying with us, they were not assuming any of the household responsibilities. Her evenings were spent cleaning the house and planning the next day's menu for us. Often it was midnight before she finally went to bed, and then she was up at five o'clock the next morning getting ready to go back to the hospital. She arrived between seven-thirty and eight for her shift, and my father, who had spent a miserable night in a chair, left to drive across town to feed his twenty horses. Afterwards, he changed into a suit and then drove to his office where he spent the day working.

Both of my parents grew so completely exhausted on this schedule that towards the end, each was falling asleep while driving on the freeway. My father's job was a demanding one under the best of circumstances, and the added stress of his son's illness put him under almost unbearable pressure. One evening he asked us children to join together and pray for Israel's recovery. When we had finished, Dad broke into tears and sobbed, "My baby is dying!" It was the only time I have ever seen Dad cry, and I was so shocked and affected by the scene that I still recall it clearly.

Dad probably suffered almost as much as Israel did. He was present on several occasions when it looked as if Israel were in his death throes, and for him this was torture. Thirty-six hours after the initial surgery a second operation was performed to remove the gangrenous portion of the bowel. Israel's condition was so deteriorated that the surgeon told my parents to prepare themselves for his death.

Miraculously, Israel survived the operation, but he was barely alive when he was returned to his room. Dad sent Mother home to prepare for her shift the following day and took up his vigil by Israel's bedside. Years later, the memory of that horrible night still stood out in Dad's mind as he repeated to us the terrifying spectacle he witnessed:

> A male nurse had accompanied Israel to the room. He had long dirty hair which was fastened at the nape of his neck with a rubber band, and his unkept beard and moustache gave him an altogether unsavory appearance. He was the antithesis of the starched white "angel of mercy" I had hoped would attend my son. My first thought was that nursing had deteriorated a great deal to allow a person such as this to work on a pediatric ward. Minutes later, however, I

was grateful that this young man had been assigned to my child.

It became apparent that this nurse was unusually efficient. He adjusted the tubes and took Israel's temperature, and although these were ordinary enough tasks, he accomplished them with a skill I had not seen in the other nurses. Then, as he prepared to suction Israel's mouth, Israel's body convulsed violently. A gurgling noise came from his throat, and a geyser of blood spewed from his lips. Israel then fell backward on the pillow forcing the blood back down his throat.

I was standing on the side of the bed opposite the nurse holding onto the guard rail. I now found myself gripping the rail for support as my knees turned to water and the strength drained from my legs. In seconds the bed sheets and pillow were a soggy red mass, and I believed that I was witnessing the death of my son.

The nurse neither looked up nor spoke. He was holding the suction tube with one hand and Israel's face with the other. With lightening-like speed he suctioned Israel's throat and mouth. I could not bear to watch my baby die, and I turned my face toward the wall.

Moments later, when I forced my eyes back to the scene in the bed, I was amazed to see that Israel was still breathing evenly and that the nurse had completely cleared his air passages and cleaned his face. For the first time the nurse spoke, "That was blood that had collected in his stomach during surgery." Those were the only words he spoke to me that night, and he never looked at me. I did not see that young man again, but I knew that his efficiency and alertness had prevented my child from drowning in his own blood.

I learned something very important that night. I had judged this nurse's ability solely on the basis of physical appearance. I promised that never again would I make this same error, and I never have.

As for Mother, during the entire ordeal, I never saw her shed a tear, but I could see the strain in her eyes, and I knew that worry and exhaustion were taking their toll. I later learned that during the time that she was at the hospital, she held Israel on her lap every moment, never putting him down unless a nurse had to work with him. Because he was connected to tubes which came out with the slightest movement, holding him meant sitting perfectly still for hours on end. Once she held him this way for twelve hours, rising only once when a nurse came to check him. She did not eat anything during that time because Israel could be fed only through an I.V., and she could not bear to eat in front of him when he was so hungry for solid food. Yet, although she deprived herself of food and comfort, she did not go without school. Every day she took one of my high school books with her and spent the day reading. In fact, it was during this time that she read *Wuthering Heights* which had been assigned as part of my English literature course.

The doctors did not believe that Israel would survive, but many prayers were going up for him during this time. When at last my parents were able to bring him home, he was still violently ill. He required a special diet, much rest, and constant care. Even with these difficulties, however, the day after she brought him home, Mother put all of us back in school. In the months that followed, though she had to take Israel nearly once a week for doctor's appointments and constantly monitor him, she managed to teach us our lessons every day.

When the "experts" had predicted that Israel would suffer severe health problems until he was a teenager, they had not counted on the power of prayer. In the months that followed Israel's release from the hospital, his face looked like a death mask. Friends were startled to see that his eyes were sunken and had lost their luster, and his body was emaciated. The skin hung in loose folds on his bony frame. Whenever I looked at him, I was reminded of the photographs I had seen of Jews in the Nazi death camps. It appeared as if each day might be his last, but somehow he managed to hold on.

However, Mother was determined that her son would not only survive but that he would regain perfect health. She prayed for him day and night, and she became a wall of protection for him, preparing special foods for him, gently bathing his withered body and even holding him in her lap and feeding him as if he were an infant. Still, she was never satisfied -- she wanted a miracle, and she knew that only God can perform miracles.

Mother was beginning to drive the other members of the family crazy. We were grateful that Israel was alive. We could not understand why she was not willing to accept the doctors' diagnosis and wait for time to heal him. One night we were watching "The 700 Club" on television and the host began to pray for the sick. Once again Mother lept to her feet and ran to Israel's room. She came back carrying the sleeping child in her arms. As she seated herself on the couch she declared, "This is it. Israel is going to be healed tonight."

We had been recruited to pray for Israel's healing a hundred times before, but obediently Dad and I gathered around him and placed our hands on his pitiful little body. Israel never awoke, and this prayer appeared to be no different from the others, but when we had finished, Mother seemed satisfied.

After she returned the slumbering child to his bed, she rejoined us in the den. She was exuberant! "Israel is healed!" she declared.

"That's wonderful," responded my father. "Maybe now you will let us have a little peace and quiet around here."

From that moment Mother believed that Israel was well, and two weeks later her convictions were confirmed by the pediatrician. When Dr. Ayo entered the examining room, he stopped dead in his tracks, and for a few moments he remained speechless as he stared at his young patient.

"What happened to Israel?" he asked.

"He's well," Mother replied.

"I can see that," the doctor responded. "How did he get that way?"

"Well," Mother began, "about two weeks ago. . ."

By September of 1982, just nine months after his surgery, Israel was completely well. His healing had been as miraculous as it had been complete. Three years old, he was no longer visiting his doctor, was taking no medication, and was able to eat a regular diet! Every time I saw him running and playing with the other children, I was thankful that God had spared his life and restored him to perfect health.

Amid these disruptions, school had remained a constant, yet now it, too, was changing. Months before, my parents had realized that I would be graduating from the American School in June and would be ready to begin my studies with a university. However, they also realized that it would not be wise to send me to a traditional university at this point. Among eighteen and twenty year olds, I would be considered a freak. Too young to date or go to parties, I would be something of a "fifth wheel." These people, six or eight years older than I, could not possibly relate to me as an equal or accept me as their peer. Such an arrangement would be terrible for me emotionally.

Besides, my parents felt that I would be exposed to unsavory influences on a typical college campus. A major reason that my parents had embarked on this program in the first place was to shelter us from destructive peer pressure while instilling their own values and principles. They had, consequently, taken great pains to teach us temperance, self-discipline, respect for authority, and faith in Christ. They feared that on a traditional university campus where I might be exposed to obscene language, drug and alcohol use, sexual promiscuity, and rebellion against authority, all of their years of labor and sacrifice would be sabotaged. Perhaps at eighteen or nineteen, when my own values had been firmly established, I could enter such an environment and still hold fast to the principles I had learned at home, but not at twelve.

A number of alternatives which would keep me active during the years until I would be old enough to "go off to college" were discussed. These included the possibility of having a rabbi come to our house certain days each week to teach me to read and write Hebrew. While this seemed like a good supplement to my education, my parents did not like the idea of my having to wait several years to complete an education on which i had such an excellent beginning.

Ideally, Mother and Dad hoped to find a university through which I could earn a bachelor's degree in my home, but they had no assurance that any such institution existed. However, through inquiry they had managed to locate excellent elementary and secondary schools, and they felt that they owed it to themselves to at least attempt to find a suitable university.

Since Harry Marcoplis had been able to recommend the American School, my father consulted him about finding a university program. Marcoplis was aware of no programs which offered degrees through correspondence, but he suggested that my parents consider enrolling me in a program for gifted young people through Johns Hopkins University. He assured my parents that he could arrange to have me admitted to the program. The only drawback was that I would have to go to Maryland to live on campus, and this was precisely what my parents were trying to avoid.

Back at square one, we next contacted the American School. Although they could not recommend an institution, they advised us to order a copy of Peterson's Guides, *Who Offers Part Time Degree Programs?* When the book arrived, however, Mother was dismayed to find that it was a 292 page catalogue of universities alphabetized under their home states. Moreover, we later discovered that not all universities listed actually offer courses through correspondence and that only a handful offer degrees. She realized that by the time she had contacted every university in this book, I would be old enough to attend college on campus!

Still, she had to start somewhere, and so, with a prayer on her lips, she let the catalogue fall open at random. To her surprise, the entry on the page before her read, "Brigham Young University," and the description underneath said that the school offered an external degree program. My parents were instantly intrigued. They were well aware of the impressive reputation enjoyed by BYU, and they knew that a degree from such a university would be above question. Immediately, they contacted the school about enrolling me.

My father made the initial telephone inquiry and was referred to Drs. Ralph Rowley and Frank Santiago, both from the university's Department of Continuing Education. These two gentlemen appeared rather incredulous when told that my father had an eleven (soon to be twelve) year-old-daughter who was about to graduate high school and wanted to enroll in the Degrees by Independent Study Program. At six o'clock the following morning, Dr. Rowley called my mother to discuss her feelings about enrolling me at such a young age.

In order to assure the faculty that they were not the victims of an elaborate practical joke, Mother wrote a lengthy letter explaining her preference for home-schooling and outlining her goals for her children. The letter also assured them that I had never skipped a grade in school, and was nearing my high school graduation. In addition, she instructed me to make a cassette tape, outlining my own goals and aspirations. Later, at my graduation, one of the DIS secretaries presented me with this tape, which had apparently been lost in my file, and only recently rediscovered. It was ironic that during my last week as a student at BYU, I was able to hear a recording of my initial contact with my alma mater. On the tape I mentioned that it was my desire to "earn a law degree and eventually to become a judge," and that a bachelor's degree was critical to realizing my goals.

Dr. Rowley responded to our application in a letter stating, "I can't help but be touched by the dedication you have for your children's well-being, and for the efforts you are going to in order to provide them with the Christian background you are giving them in their education. I believe that you will find the environment at BYU in harmony with the Christian ethics you are striving for in your family." Rowley requested copies of my grade transcripts from the American School but promised to go ahead and send my enrollment forms. "With Alexandra's background," he concluded, "I am confident that she can complete the Bachelor of Independent Studies program at an accelerated rate." (His prediction was fulfilled -- I completed all of my course work within two years and nine months after beginning the program.)

The American School forwarded the requested transcripts, and after reviewing my grades, the administration seemed satisfied. However, I was later informed that my enrollment went all the way to the vice president's office for approval.

Although my parents had contacted BYU before I actually graduated from the American School, it was September of 1982 before I began my studies. I was either too immature or too naive to be nervous about beginning university work, for I felt that as long as I had my tutor at my side, I could not really go wrong. Besides, I never believed that anything was unattainable to me or that any task was too difficult. As far as I was concerned, I could handle my studies at the university as well as any adult.

I believe that Mother was far more anxious, although she never said or did anything to let me know that she had any doubts. Always before, she had been tutoring me at levels with which she was familiar. She had never attended college, however, and together she and I were about to break new ground.

Moreover, the Degrees by Independent Study program is designed to benefit adults who are beyond the traditional age for college attendance, and consequently, it assumes a certain amount of "life experience" on the part of the student. Ironically, rather than being enrolled in a program for gifted young students, as Harry Marcoplis had suggested, I had landed in a program where the average age of my classmates was forty-two. None-the-less, the university was adamant that they were making no exceptions for me -- I would either conform to their standards or I was out.

The DIS program, which requires 128 units for graduation, is designed to provide the student with a liberal arts degree. Unlike most other baccalaureate programs, it does not offer a major. Instead, the student works through five different areas of study. These include the areas of English and logic, the arts, sciences, world religions, and social sciences. Each of these areas of study is followed by a two week seminar on campus during which the student has the opportunity to attend lectures by the professors through whom he has been working at home and to interact with other students in the program. Testing also takes place during these seminars. In addition, at the completion of the program, each student is required to prepare a 50-75 page paper on a subject of his choice, and finally to make an oral presentation of his paper on campus the week before graduation.

On my first day as a "college girl," I arrived at the dining table at eight-thirty with my books in hand and my syllabus open. I was both excited and curious about the prospect of college, and I wondered what I might expect from my new school. Mother sat down with me, and together we looked over my first unit of study -- Foundations -- a thirteen lesson course in basic English and logic. We spent a couple of days discussing my first assignment, a five-hundred word essay on "My Greatest Learning Experience." When I had finished the essay, we proofread and typed it.

At first, I was a little intimidated by the amount of writing I had to do in Foundations. Although I had written many compositions in Calvert and had taken three English courses in the American School, I had never written anything as long as five hundred words -- five hundred words was the shortest assignment I encountered at BYU. I soon adapted quite well, however. In some ways, Foundations was simple enough to allay some of our apprehensions, for the course concentrates on basic English and logic skills -- skills in which I was already well versed. Most assignments did not seem very difficult.

In other ways, Foundations provided me with some challenging new experiences. I was horrified to discover that the course concluded with a ten-page research paper. The essay could be on the subject of my choice, but it had to be logical, well documented -- with footnotes and a complete bibliography -- and it had to demonstrate clear, mature thought. When the initial shock of fright wore off, I chose "The Trauma of Abortion" as my subject. Researching the paper through the local Right to Life groups and Planned Parenthood, I was able to conduct interviews with both pro and anti-abortion counselors.

It was the first serious research I had done, and the first "long" paper I had written. I put heart and soul into it, and when I had finished, Mother typed it for me. When, finally, I sent it to my professor, I thought that it was nothing short of a masterpiece. While he probably did not share my enthusiasm, he apparently was pleased with the final result, because although the assignment required that all papers go through two drafts, the professors who reviewed my paper accepted it on the first submission.

Upon completion of Foundations, I was required to attend a two-week seminar on the BYU campus in Provo, Utah. The Foundations seminar takes place twice a year -- in January and in June. Because I finished Foundations in December, and because the university prefers that students attend seminars before enrolling in the next area of study, Mother enrolled me in the January seminar.

Trying to arrange our schedules around the trip proved quite a lot more difficult than the seminar itself. Dad had initially planned to take me, but at the last moment he could not leave his work; thus, on the eve of our departure Mother found herself hastily packing. The next morning as we drove to the airport there were tears in her eyes. For the first time she was leaving her eight other children for two weeks. During the day the children would have a maid to stay with them, and at night my father would be home, but even so she would worry until we could return.

As for me, every precaution had been taken to insure that I would be thoroughly prepared for this trip. Mother had spent weeks purchasing my wardrobe. She made certain that I had a different outfit for each day of the two weeks that I would be there. More importantly, she insured that I was academically prepared for the seminar.

In the syllabus were a number of "pre-seminar assignments" which were to be completed before the seminar began. Mother saw to it that I completed every lesson satisfactorily, and that all these assignments were typed and bound in folders to be taken to the school. One assignment gave the student the option of preparing either a written or an oral report. Mother insisted that I do both. Consequently, at home I prepared a written paper on "Homogenization in the Media," and also rehearsed a talk on that subject. Every time I complained about the amount of preparatory work I was having to do, my parents reminded me that I would be by far the youngest person in my class, and that I would have to work doubly hard to prove myself. With this thought in mind, and my assignments in my suitcase, I set off for Provo that dreary morning with mixed feelings of dread and enthusiasm.

"Think of this as an adventure," my father advised me. "You can make it into a good adventure or a bad adventure, depending on your attitude." I was prepared for my first venture into the great wide world to be very exciting and glamorous. After all, not only would I be setting foot on a university campus for the first time, but I would be doing so as the youngest student at the institution. If I had expected celebrity status, my illusions would soon be shattered. I would, however, encounter something much better than celebrity status at BYU; I would encounter a faculty and student body who were willing to accept me as a peer.

Mother and I arrived in Provo on a cold, bleak Sunday afternoon, thoroughly exhausted from having risen at four o'clock that morning to make the five-hour flight from El Paso, Texas to Salt Lake City, Utah, followed by an hour's drive forty miles south to Provo. Four months pregnant, Mother was wearing a black suit with high-heeled pumps, while I was dressed in a skirt and blouse with lower-heeled shoes. Waiting in our hotel room for the luggage to arrive on the shuttle, Mother suggested that she and I walk up on the campus to attempt to locate my classroom. The January air felt like ice as we began a long, fruitless trek across the hilly terrain. Only a pale glint of muted sunlight shone through the dark clouds, and since we had not been able to find the building and were certain that a storm must be approaching, we decided to return to our hotel.

Back in our warm room, we took off our shoes and relaxed while Mother called Dr. Rowley to ask him for directions so that we could find the classroom the following morning. Dr. Rowley immediately insisted upon coming by the hotel and driving us to the classroom. Although Mother assured him that this was unnecessary and that she would be happy to simply write down his instructions and follow them in the morning, he was insistent. Miserably, we forced our shoes back onto our throbbing feet. Within a few moments he and his wife had arrived and driven us to a large building complex in the center of the campus. After helping us out of the car, Rowley indicated the proper building and then said, "We have a meeting to attend so we can't stay, but I'll leave you two here to look around." Obviously, he thought that we wanted to spend some time looking around the campus, and he had no idea that both of us were exhausted, for to our amazement, he and his wife then jumped into the car and sped away, leaving us to walk the mile and a half back to our hotel. Shocked, we laughed all the way back to the room.

As we returned to the hotel that afternoon, we had a new appreciation of the BYU faculty. On a campus of twenty-six thousand students, Dr. Rowley had taken the time from a busy weekend schedule to drive a single student to the building where her classes would be held the following day. Even before the seminars began, we knew that BYU was no ordinary university, and we were certain as we walked through the cold

58

January twilight that the Lord had led us there.

The next morning I entered the classroom -- which I now had no difficulty locating -- as an ordinary university student, or at least an almost ordinary one. Few students have their mothers sit in class with them, but on my first day I was overcome with stage-fright. My "first day of school" had come seven years and twelve grades late. All at once I was horrified to find myself in totally foreign surroundings, while the only familiar face was about to leave. Therefore, although she had planned to return to the hotel for the day, I asked Mother to stay with me and, with the consent of the professors, she agreed. After the first day she seemed as much a part of the class as anyone!

As the first order of business, each of the students introduced himself and told a little about his background. I soon found that my fellow students were a curious cross-section of society. The oldest was in his fifties, while the next youngest in age to me was twenty-six. One of the men was a hunting guide from Wyoming, and one of the women was a legal secretary. Three of the older women were housewives. One student was a health food enthusiast who had written and published a health food cookbook, and one woman was an Austrian-born employee of the United Nations who was stationed in Afghanistan and had come all the way to Provo for the seminar.

None of us could be considered "typical" college students -- a fact which obviously made it easier for me to fit in. In spite of the many differences among the classmates, we all had some things in common. Few of us had been to college before. Even among the exceptions, they had not attended college in twenty or thirty years. We were all nervous and anxious to perform well. My classmates were warm, friendly, and open, and I quickly became part of a team in which ideas were exchanged and assignments were discussed.

Far from feeling like an outsider, after a few days I was totally comfortable with the other members of the class. We ate lunch together each day, and Mother and I attended a play and a ballet on campus with several of the students. The United Nations employee was staying in the same hotel as we, and the three of us ate breakfast together several mornings.

Still, there was an undeniable difference between the pressures exerted by the faculty on the other students and pressures exerted on me. If the other students felt apprehensive, at least there was no question that they "belonged," while there was tremendous doubt that I should be there at all, for in addition to my many other differences,

I was the single Baptist in a sea of Mormons. Consequently, I was forced to "earn my stripes."

During the seminar, the English professor asked me to comment on every question that he asked the other students. However, Dr. Norton always treated me with a great deal of respect, and was, in fact, one of the best professors with whom I ever worked. I never felt that he was "putting me on the spot." Rather, I believe that he wanted to be sure that I really could handle the work, and I suspect that he wanted to help me feel that I, too, belonged.

I also discovered another difference between the other members of the class and me -- I was the only student who came to the seminar with all my assignments completed. The literature sent out by the school had said that all students could expect to work very hard during their two week stay, and that there would probably not be sufficient time for visits with family and friends. Mother took that statement at face value. She was thoroughly expecting me to have to work until the wee hours of every morning.

However, we soon discovered that much of the work consisted of completing the pre-seminar assignments which had posed special problems. During the seminar, the students had an opportunity to discuss these problems with the professors, and evenings and weekends were devoted to finishing any incomplete assignments. Although I had to work very hard during the classes, I did not have the added burden of dealing with incomplete assignments. While many of my fellow students were sitting up until two and three o'clock in the morning trying to finish their pre-seminar assignments and searching for topics for their library research papers, I was finished at five o'clock every afternoon when the class ended.

As a result, I found that I had a good deal of free time during the two weeks. Much of this time I enjoyed just being alone with Mother, for as the oldest of eight children, I seldom had a chance to spend time alone with her at home. Every evening when the classes ended, she and I walked in the freezing twilight back to our hotel. Being from El Paso, we were accustomed to a clear sky and relatively warm weather even in the winter, and we were rather dismayed to find that it either snowed, rained, or drizzled every day. When the weather was really inclement we took a taxi, but after a long day of sitting in class we generally preferred to walk. Back at the hotel, we went to the restaurant where a table next to the fireplace was always waiting for us. After a warm dinner, we returned to our comfortable room where we spent the evening watching television or talking.

On Saturday it snowed -- a rare treat for me, for at home we consider snow a delightful, extraordinary event. Fortunately, we had no classes that day. We decided to accept the invitation of Kyle and Wendy Farr, a young, newlywed couple, who were both enrolled in the DIS program, to drive us to Salt Lake City for a tour of Temple Square. As neither of us had ever visited either the city or the Temple, we both greatly enjoyed ourselves. Having seen many of the city's most important religious and historical monuments, by six o'clock that evening, we were ready to return to our hotel. That day which we spent with our new friends is one of my fondest memories of BYU.

There were two major tasks which I actually had to complete at the seminar. One involved writing an in-class paper. The other was giving the talk that Mother had insisted I prepare. When the day came for the classmembers who had chosen to do so to make their oral presentations, Dr. Norton informed us that the talks would be presented over a period of two days. He then asked someone to volunteer to speak first. When the adults hesitated, I, anxious to be through with my talk after being forced to rehearse it every night in the hotel room, stepped forward.

To my surprise, I was completely relaxed, and I began to understand the value of years of oral compositions in Calvert and the speech course I had taken in the American School. Although I was speaking before a roomful of relative strangers, I felt no different than I had when making presentations at home. I also realized that I would be able to forgive Mother for forcing me to rehearse every night. When I had finished, my classmates told me that they regretted my having volunteered to speak first, because I would be a "tough act to follow." Their praise was reassuring to me, and it gave me confidence in my own ability to "hold my own" against adults in a college environment.

At last the two weeks drew to an end. The seminar concluded with a dinner for the Foundations students. We had been told that two of the students -- one man and one woman -- would be chosen to make some remarks to the rest of the class at the banquet. I was pleased to discover that I had not been chosen, although Mother had made me rehearse a speech for this occasion also -- "just in case. . ."

The next morning we were instructed to come back to the classroom for "wrap up." At eleven, when the last goodbye had been said, Mother and I caught our flight from Salt Lake City back to El Paso. How wonderful it seemed, after being rained on for two weeks in Utah, to look up into the clear West Texas sky and see the stars twinkling above us.

Immediately after my return from Provo in February, 1983, I was enrolled in my second area of study, Man and Beauty, which includes literature, music, visual arts, and theatre arts. About this time, the American School sent me a letter stating that because of my excellent grades I qualified to apply for a scholarship to be used toward my current studies in the university. The letter stated that two $1000.00 scholarships and ten $400.00 scholarships would be awarded. My parents urged me to apply. The school soon mailed me application forms and a test to be administered by a proctor under controlled circumstances. Mother arranged for the principal of a Catholic school to administer the test. A few weeks later, the American School informed me that I was the recipient of the R.T. Miller scholarship in the amount of $1000.00 and that they would be contacting BYU about how best to apply it.

The scholarship helped immensely. The tuitions for each of the five units of study cost about five hundred dollars and the fee for the seminars was about four hundred dollars each. Only Foundations cost a little less -- the seminar cost around two hundred dollars and the unit around three hundred. These prices do not include the several hundred dollars worth of books we had to buy for each course. The costs soon mounted -- particularly as my younger brother and sister began to move into the ranks of the college-bound.

My new school kept me very busy. One assignment might require me to read several books and then write two 1000-word papers. After I became accustomed to the workload, however, I did not object to the lengthy assignments. I worked from eight-thirty until eleven-thirty each morning, and from one o'clock until two o'clock each afternoon; yet, I still finished an assignment every one to two weeks, sometimes less depending on its length. As I matured emotionally and became more familiar with the expectations of my professors, I could skim one hundred pages in a few hours, and write a five-page essay in one setting.

I even learned to type well. Mother began teaching me to type when I entered the university, but during the time that I was learning, she typed my papers for me. After a few months, however, I was typing my own assignments, and by the time I was ready to graduate I could turn out five pages of typewritten, ready-to-be-submitted work in one hour.

Yet, although Mother encouraged me to work quickly, speed was never a substitute for quality. In my house, an A is excellent, A— is fair, B is poor, B— is very poor, and C is disgraceful. Consequently, she closely monitored my work to make certain that I was earning mostly A's and A—'s, with as few B's as possible. She continued to read all of my books and to personally look over my assignments. Further, after I wrote each essay, she read it critically before it was typed, and then again after it had been typed. After my assignments had been returned to me by my professors, Mother always looked at the grade herself, and read any comments which they might have written on them. As usual, she had to sandwich this work in among her other duties. Regardless of how busy she might be, though, she continued to give me the attention and supervision I needed.

I soon found that I was able to complete university work with very little difficulty. I realized as I began my studies at BYU how well my tutor and my former schools had prepared me. Calvert and the American School had familiarized me with much of the art, literature, theatre, history, and even science and math which I would encounter in the university. For example, when I attended the Man and Beauty seminar, during one lecture our literature professor discussed the Battle of Hastings. In vain I tried to recall the incident until Dr. Hunsaker mentioned the date 1066. Instantly, the name "William the Conqueror" came to mind, and I recalled that in Calvert I had been required to memorize that name in connection with the date 1066 A.D. I was immediately able to bring to mind the details of the Battle of Hastings and from then on could follow my professor's lecture without difficulty.

I had classmates who talked of the many telephone calls they made to their professors asking for assistance. During the entire time that I was in BYU I never called any of my professors to ask for help. Each morning I read my assignment from my syllabus and began working. If I did have questions, Mother was always available, but even her assistance was becoming less and less necessary. It was not unusual for me to begin an assignment, read the material, and write the paper without ever asking her a question. Yet, we continued to discuss my work.

Some of our best talks occurred when we were cooking dinner together, running errands in the car, or simply relaxing. During these times we discussed papers which had to be written or assigned reading material which we had both read. While our conversations were usually informal, they were very productive. Mother provided wonderful feedback for my ideas, and often I left our chats with a deeper understanding of my studies. One often hears stories of the self-assured young adult who comes home from college feeling much smarter than his parents. In my case, the opposite was true -- as I worked through my studies at the university, I gained an increasing appreciation of Mother's understanding and insight.

As for my father, who was in charge of every other aspect of my life, he did not interfere much in school, but he always took a great interest in what I was doing. Sometimes I felt that he was more enthused about my accomplishments than I. We always discussed in depth any project on which I happened to be working. He read my more important papers and always provided advice and input. I was pleased that he took an interest in my work, for I needed to feel that he cared about those things which were important to me.

Yet, some difficulties arose in college which required more than just the interest and concern of my parents. One of these difficult areas was music -- which comprised one-fourth of the Man and Beauty area of study. Neither of my parents has any musical training, nor can they read music or play instruments. Naturally, I knew no more about the discipline than they. Therefore, we were somewhat at a loss when we saw that my course required me to be able to count meter and determine the texture, tempo, melodic line, melodic intervals, and the tonality of the pieces. I also was required to recognize the period in which each selection was composed, the name of the composer, and the name of the composition. On selections from opera I had to be able to give the name of the opera, and the voice type of each of the performers in the selection. Further, I was often required to name some of the instruments used in certain excerpts and the elements of music employed. Nothing in my previous education had prepared me to make the distinction between a soprano and a contralto, or a recitative and an aria.

Fortunately, my parents had a friend who taught high school orchestra, and he consented to help. Evening after evening was spent on the telephone as he taught me the basics I needed to complete the course. Each morning I would try to apply the essentials I had learned the night before. Needless to say, I spent many frustrating hours, and at some points I felt that I was not ever going to learn anything this way. Obviously, much of what I did learn I was forced to more or less figure out for myself, for it is very difficult to receive comprehensive instruction in music over the telephone. In spite of these handicaps, I made remarkably good grades -- my average for the course was an A—.

The following year I had an opportunity to determine how much I really had learned when I helped tutor Christopher through music. To my surprise, I actually remembered more than I would have thought. How well I passed on my knowledge I cannot be sure, but I know that he, too, averaged an A— for the course.

However, the true test of our knowledge, or perhaps our tenacity, came at the Man and Beauty seminar, which included two music tests. The first test required that we be able to define over one hundred common musical terms and state the language from which each originated. We also were required to complete a circle of fifths -- a musical device listing all of the notes in sharps and flats. Mother invented a simple means for memorizing the circle of fifths, and Christopher and I memorized the terms and their definitions in a couple of days. Thus, this test proved simple.

The second test was much more complicated. In one hour, we heard fifteen selections played, each for a period of three minutes. As each selection played, we were supposed to fill in the name of the composer, the period during which it was composed, and other similar information. Chris and I spent every free moment during the seminar studying for that test. We listened to selection after selection on the cassette tapes sent with the course in order to learn to identify the various aspects of the music. When the day finally came for the test, the pressure on the class was terrific. For one hour we sweated through the almost impossible task of filling out the required information on the chart with the selections still playing. We breathed a sigh of relief when the test was finally completed, although we did not see our grade for several days.

When our papers were returned to us, we learned that Christopher and I were two of the three highest scorers. Dr. Halliday may have sensed that we were under special pressure, because he called us aside and told us that he was very pleased that we had performed so well in his class at our ages. (I was fourteen and Christopher was thirteen.) After having been under so much strain for so long, the compliment was much appreciated.

The following year, Mother had the opportunity to meet Dr. Halliday at my Closure seminar. During their brief conversation she mentioned that music had been very difficult for us because we had no musical training. Halliday was incredulous! He said that he could not believe that we had performed so well at the seminar without being able to read music. In truth, I was as surprised as he.

Dr. James Rawson, who later replaced Ralph Rowley as the director of the Degrees by Independent Study program, once attributed our success to "the way they are being raised, and God-given ability." Although ability was a factor, I feel that our upbringing played a much greater role in our success at BYU. Our home-schooling experiences have forced us to work for so many years without much outside help that, when confronted with a difficult problem, our first response is to sit down and attempt to work through it.

This unusual situation has helped all of us to learn to be self-starters. Even Mother, who has always been independent, has developed an even greater sense of independence since she embarked on this endeavor. Not long ago we purchased our first home computer. Neither Mother nor any of us children had ever seen a computer close-up, and we had absolutely no idea how to operate one. However, after five years of constant use our typewriter was no longer producing high-quality work, and Mother wanted the children who were in the university to begin using the computer for their essays as quickly as possible (I had already graduated). Therefore, Mother spent an entire weekend figuring out how to use the computer. We discovered that the instruction manual which came with the machine had been written for several models of the same brand of computer and that following the manual step-by-step often led us absolutely nowhere. Mother made two trips and several phone calls to Radio Shack, where the computer had originated, to learn enough to get started. She then sat down and spent many hours over the next several days figuring out how to get into different programs, how to use the printer, and how to enter text. Within three weeks, with virtually no assistance or instruction, we had learned enough to produce two very professional-looking contracts, a spread sheet for my father's business, and several short papers for school.

This sense of independence and self-reliance is apparent among many home-school families. In fact, a friend of mine who is a writer recently told me that home-school families are more likely to start their own businesses than other families because they are accustomed to doing things for themselves. While I cannot attest to the accuracy of this statement, I do know that in our case home-schooling has definitely resulted in a sense of self-confidence and self-reliance among the members of our family.

By September of 1983, I had matured a great deal from the girl I had been the previous year. I was firmly established in a new school where I was earning good grades and enjoying academic and intellectual experiences which escape most other teenagers. In addition, I was learning to be independent and to rely on my own abilities. It seemed that I had everything any child could want. Yet, though my childhood seemed close to perfect, I was not to escape the "growing pains" which are a part of life.

Shortly after I began high school: Left to right, Victoria at five, Francesca at seven, me at ten.

Back row: Dominic at age six.
Front row: Christopher at nine, Israel at one year, Benjamin at three.

Mother and Dad just after their marriage in 1963.

Mother and Dad in 1970, shortly before I was born.

Just before I entered BYU, Francesca at eight, Victoria at six and me at eleven.

Israel around the time of his second surgery.

Francesca

Left to right: Dominic, Christopher.

Dominic

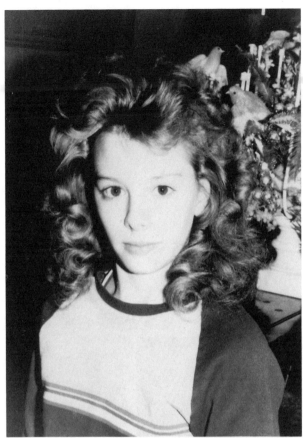

Victoria

Benjamin

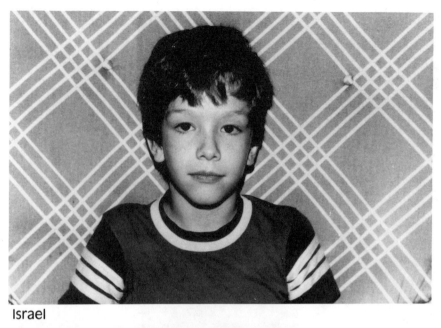

Israel

Gabrielle

Left to right: Judah, Stefan.

Dad shortly after
I began college.

Mother the year I graduated from BYU.

Mother and me on the BYU campus for Closure Week 1986.

Mother and me on the BYU campus for Closure Week 1986.

Standing next to the statue of Brigham Young for my graduation picture. A friend insisted on renting the cap and gown for the photo.

FIVE
"TRAIN UP A CHILD. . ."

Most people who have not been involved in home-schooling have images of the home-schooled child living his life in an ivory tower, surrounded only by books, food and water, cut off from all human contact from birth until adulthood. Therefore, they believe that he grows up to be a lonely, maladjusted, poorly educated, introverted, social misfit. In reality, nothing could be further from the truth. The home-schooled child often has a very positive self-image because he has always been treated as an individual rather than merely "part of the crowd." He is accustomed to being related to on a one-on-one basis. Therefore, he rarely feels that he must do something to make himself "stand out." He often feels that he is special, a person of value who has a contribution to make to the world. Consequently, because he respects himself, he is able to show the same respect for others and to engage in lasting relationships.

In my opinion, home-schooling provides the best possible socialization for a child. According to *Webster's New Collegiate Dictionary,* to socialize is "to fit or train for a social environment." Proper socialization does not merely entail being able to establish friendships with people of similar age, religious persuasion, ethnic background and socio-economic status. Rather, true socialization is learning to relate to people very different from oneself.

Many parents find that home-schooling allows their children to achieve this type of socialization. Through home-schooling the parent is able to provide his child with the tools he will need in order to relate to people on a variety of levels. The first step is often to clearly establish the identity of the child. The home-schooling parent often wants his child to have a firmly established set of values and to know what is expected of him, so that when confronted with peer pressure he will stand his ground. In most cases this does not mean that the parent wishes to prevent his child from having any social contacts. It merely means that the parent does not want the child to feel that he can establish his own identity only through association with others.

Home-schooling is unique in that it preserves the family values -- it allows the parent the rare opportunity to instill his own principles in his child without outside interference. Parents and children involved in home-schooling spend a great deal more time together than they would under other circumstances, and it is easy for the parent to introduce instruction beyond that of the textbook. In addition, the home-schooled child is accustomed to seeing his parent in the role of teacher, and therefore, he accepts and respects his parents' ideas. The parent can also insure that his child's friends and social contacts will share similar values and beliefs, thus reinforcing the lessons the child is learning at home.

Most home-school families belong to support groups where they meet other children and parents involved in similar programs. My family was unusual in that our contacts were much more limited. We did not belong to any support group, and we lived in the country where we did not really have neighbors. Yet, my parents took great pains to insure that we did not escape "socialization." Our childhoods were spent in preparation for the day when we would enter the mainstream of society.

The Bible commends parents to "Train up a child in the way he should go and when he is old he will not depart from it." Therefore, Mother and Dad began our spiritual training long before they began our scholastic training. From the day I was born, each day my parents read four chapters from the Old Testament and two chapters from the New Testament to me. The text they used was the Living Bible, which is written in contemporary English, but for adults rather than children, and they read straight through from Genesis to Revelations. Mother kept a bookmark in each of the Testaments so that she would know where to start reading every day. I was not permitted to play, talk, or make noise during these readings, but was expected to listen quietly and attentively.

This practice continues in our home to this day and has served through the years not only to provide religious instruction, but to teach us other skills as well. As a result of these readings, the attention span and ability to concentrate of even the youngest children in the family have been vastly improved. In addition, the readings have helped to expand the children's vocabularies, since the Bible is a fairly complex book.

Teaching us to relate properly to others also meant enforcing discipline and curbing our undesirable traits. My parents always insisted that we show them complete respect, never allowing us to "talk back" or raise our voices to them. If we had an opinion or an objection, we could voice it -- but only in a dignified, respectful manner. They also insisted that we treat one another with dignity and respect. Fighting was not allowed, nor could we verbally assault one another. "Remember," Mother reminded us, "other people have feelings too." We were forced to be polite -- even when angry -- with the result that we settled most of our differences quickly. This, too, was an important part of socialization, for we were learning to resolve our own little conflicts. The experiences prepared us to deal with other social situations as we grew older.

By the time I was thirteen years old my parents had ten children, and I spent most of my time with my brothers and sisters. I helped to feed the smaller ones their bottles, and I changed their diapers and baby-sat when Mother and Dad went out. I was learning to share authority and responsibility with my siblings closest to me in age.

We had always enjoyed one another immensely. Even when we were four and five years old we played together constantly, usually finding a way to incorporate even the youngest child into our games. Mother tells me that once when my brother Dominic was about three months old, she heard Christopher, Francesca and me yelling, "Stray dog! Help!" at the tops of our voices. Alarmed, she rushed into the room where we were playing to find us circling the blanket on which Dominic was lying while he stared at us in horror. We had decided to play a game involving a stray dog, and he, as the youngest member of the family, had been forced to assume the role.

Mother says that one of the nice things about having a large family is that when one of the children is angry with one or two of the others he can play with someone else until he "cools down." In our case, we always had someone with whom to play.

In fact, there are so many children that they tend to associate with one another in little groups according to their ages. Christopher, Francesca, and Dominic are virtually inseparable. They share a love for animals, professional sports, board games and music. Benjamin and Israel are equally close. Because they are both boys and only fourteen months apart in age, they really enjoy each other's company. Stefan and Judah are also close. I have often walked into the room to find them sitting with their arms around each other, talking softly. The four smallest boys share a room, giving them more opportunity to spend time together. One morning, Judah told Mother that he and his brothers love to lie in bed and watch the sunrise while they tell each other their dreams from the night before.

Victoria and Gabrielle are in between, and so they intermingle among groups. Victoria and Francesca spend much of their time together, and since all children over ten years old are allowed to stay up until nine o'clock on school nights, Victoria spends most evenings playing cards and board games with Francesca, Christopher and Dominic. However, she also plays outside with the younger six. Gabrielle, a single girl sandwiched in among four boys, plays and roughhouses just as they do. When she is in the mood for more ladylike play, she has Victoria for a companion, and she is also very close to Francesca.

As the oldest, I am close to all of them, though in different ways. My brothers and sisters closest to me in age make up for the teenage contacts I lack outside my family. They are my best friends. Our fundamental beliefs and perceptions are identical, and we share the same sense of humor. Therefore, we can talk about almost everything. Not only can we share problems with one another, but we can help to keep each other laughing. Francesca is a notorious tease with a wonderful sense of humor, who knows just what to say to keep everyone in his or her place. Dominic loves to mimic television personalities, with hysterical results. Even Christopher, who appears on the surface to be very serious, possesses a zany personality.

The younger children seem more like nieces and nephews than brothers and sisters. In them I see something of myself when I was their ages, and they never fail to amaze and amuse me. I have had the opportunity to help Mother a little by teaching them some of their assignments, and the experiences have been ones I have immensely enjoyed. I find that their perspective is often totally different from mine. They pose questions or make comments which would never enter my mind. My life would be very lonely without my large, bustling family.

Still, I had to learn to adjust to differences in my family. We have twelve distinct personalities living under one roof, and some disagreements and conflicts are natural. Learning to overcome such conflicts and to respect the differences between oneself and others is an important part of healthful socialization. One of the most important factors I had to overcome in developing good relationships with my brothers and sisters was my feeling of competition with them. Sibling rivalry was particularly strong where my sister Francesca was concerned. Although we should have been good friends, since we were so close in age, somehow I always felt very threatened by her. After all, I had been around first, and I did not feel that I should have to share the limelight with my younger sister. I was afraid that she would turn out to be smarter, or prettier, or more popular than I. As we got older, people began to confuse us with one another, which, for me, only compounded the problem. I was my own distinct person and did not wish to be mistaken for my sister. My feelings resulted in a number of clashes, over which I nearly always felt guilty afterward, for Francesca was very sweet to me no matter how nasty I became. However, I did not feel guilty enough to reform, and most of the trouble I got into as a child was the result of arguing with my sister.

It is said that you can pick your friends but not your family. Had Francesca and I been raised differently, we might never have resolved our conflicts. We probably would have developed friendships with other people and ignored one another. In our particular situation, however, this really was not possible. If I wanted a female friend my own age, I was going to have to swallow my pride and make peace with Francesca. For several years I was unwilling to do this, but as we became teenagers we began to overcome some of our disagreements. We began to develop our own distinct interests and identities, and to become comfortable with who we are. As we did so, we learned to respect each other and to find points of common interest. We might not always have the same taste, but deep down Francesca and I are very much alike, and we have much to offer one another.

We also learned to compromise and accept our differences. For her thirteenth birthday, Francesca received a radio on which she likes to play country western music in our bedroom. I, personally, am not fond of country music, but I have learned to accept it without complaint and to let her play what she likes. One of the most important lessons that I learned is that there is nothing wrong with being different from my sister. Merely because I may prefer to stay inside and bake or read, while she plays outside with our dog, or runs races with the boys, does not mean that we cannot be close. Although it has taken quite a few years, Francesca and I have finally learned to appreciate one another, and we now enjoy a very good relationship. We have each been able to find our own space, to become comfortable with who we are, and to become comfortable with each other.

Finding one's own niche is very important to becoming comfortable with oneself and others. In our house, every child has his own space which he fills, his own role that he alone occupies. From birth my parents told each of us that we were special, and that no one could ever take our place; yet, school was also instrumental in helping us establish ourselves. An excellent example is my six-year-old brother Stefan.

At the age of three, when most children have already mastered their verbal skills, Stefan refused to talk. Judah, who is ten months younger than he, was talking, but Stefan would not. My parents pleaded, cajoled, and offered bribes, completely without success. Still, he could communicate amazingly well.

Once when one of the older children hit Stefan, he decided to tell Mother about it. Entering the room where she was working, he tapped her shoulder to get her attention. Then he proceeded to pantomime a choking. "Someone choked you?" Mother, who had learned to interpret these signs, asked. Stefan nodded affirmatively. Next, he hit himself in the stomach and then doubled over, indicating that his assailant had also punched him in the stomach. "Who did this to you?" Mother asked. Stefan's face fell, but he remained silent. "If you will tell me who hit you, I will punish them," Mother promised. Still, there was no response. Finally, she began to say the name of each child in the family, and when she came to the right one, Stefan nodded.

Even though he could not be persuaded to talk, my parents felt that Stefan possessed verbal skills because he could imitate sounds. One evening Mother heard the dog howling unusually loudly. She walked to the back door to tell it to be quiet, when to her surprise she discovered that the dog was not responsible for the noise at all. Stefan was sitting by the back door imitating the dog's howl perfectly.

Finally, Mother and Dad took Stefan to a doctor to determine whether there might be a physical problem. After examining him thoroughly, the pediatrician concluded that there was nothing physically wrong with Steffy. "He is very bright," the doctor told my parents, explaining that very bright children often talk either unusually early or unusually late. In Stefan's case, refusal to talk was a way of forcing my parents to give him extra attention. "He'll talk when he's ready," concluded the doctor. My parents returned home not much comforted.

The turning point came when Judah began receiving so much attention because he did talk. Stefan's resistance finally broke and he, too, began to speak. Even after he began talking, however, he often seemed grumpy and out of sorts. When he was in a good mood, he was the most winsome child I have ever known, but unfortunately he was seldom in a good mood. Although he was an obedient child, he seemed full of pent up frustration -- perhaps at having been born the second youngest child in a family of ten. I feared that he would be a terrible problem when he started school, for he can be horribly stubborn, and I believed he would simply refuse to cooperate.

The day he started school, however, the most remarkable change came over him. He positively beamed with happiness and contentment. I had never seen him look so pleased for such a long period of time. He proudly displayed his school box to everyone, and that night he joyfully announced to Dad, "I'm a Calvert boy now!"

However, on the second day, in the middle of his studies, he suddenly burst into tears. Sobbing, he told Mother that he was tired of school and that he wanted to quit. Mother gently put her arms around him and explained that all little boys have to go to school and that he could not quit his studies after the first day. In a few moments the scene was over, the tears were dried, and he was ready to resume. Since that day he always says that he loves school, and he behaves as though he means it. In the evening, when my father comes home, Stefan is usually waiting with a paper to show him.

Mother believes that school has given Stefan a sense of being grown up, and also a sense of belonging. It has provided him with his own special corner where he alone belongs. Now, as she explains it, "He has his own work, which only he does. He is the only child in the fourth grade, and it sets him apart from the others." He is also in a position where Mother has to give him individual attention. She is forced to devote a few hours a day strictly to him, and he guards her attention jealously. Recently she asked me to help her in class by teaching him one of his lessons. Stefan burst into tears, saying that he did not want to be taught by anyone but Mother. Under the circumstances we felt obligated to comply with his wish, and Mother taught the lesson.

In spite of his eccentricities, however, Stefan is actually a very happy, well-adjusted child and an excellent student. In his spare time, he plays happily with his brothers and sisters and enjoys the company of his parents. He is remarkably loving and affectionate toward family members, and very outgoing with strangers.

People frequently ask me, "But what will you do when you get into the real world?" I am then tempted to ask, "What makes you think that my world is any less real than yours?" After all, reality is relative. The world of a teenage runaway is certainly not real to Nelson Rockefeller's daughter, anymore than the world of an Ethiopian who grows up, lives and dies in a famine ridden country is real to the average, middle-class American. Who is to say which of these worlds is "real," since each is so different from the others? It remains a simple fact that although all of us are aware that many different lifestyles and cultures exist on this planet, the "real world" remains the one which an individual builds for himself or which someone else builds for him. The life I enjoy may not be typical but it is most certainly real, and I can think of no better lifestyle.

In many ways my brothers and sisters have been my teachers also, for from each of them I have learned something special which will always remain with me. From Christopher, who is seventeen, I have learned the importance of confronting fears and difficulties.

When Chris was about three years old he had the daily responsibility of watering the cows we then owned. He had seen our father perform this task many times and had noted that Dad often put the water hose down any gopher hole he found in the field. One day after Chris had watered the cows, he decided to put the hose down a gopher hole that he had discovered, but upon doing so he was horrified to find that this particular hole was inhabited by five baby gophers who came scurrying up for air. Terrified, he thought that if he ran they might catch him. Therefore, Chris stood his ground and beat them with the hose. When the last gopher lay dead upon the ground, he flew into the house, explained the situation to Mother, and then added, "I was afraid that if I ran they would get me, so I whipped them until they all went to sleep."

I have always liked that story because I think it tells something very important about Christopher's personality. Ten years later, when he was fourteen, Christopher found himself in a very similar situation, except that this time the danger was very real. Mother had driven Christopher and Dominic to the farm where we keep our twenty thoroughbred horses so that the boys could feed and water the animals. As they drove up, Chris noticed a pack of wild dogs on the property. Because the farm is in a remote area, wild dogs are not an uncommon sight, and Christopher knew the danger which the animals posed to our foals and pregnant mares. Grabbing his loaded twenty-two caliber rifle, he jumped from the van and ran behind the barn to chase away the predators.

Usually wild dogs are timid, and they flee at the first sight of people, but these animals were bolder, and when Christopher ran behind the barn the pack was waiting for him. From her position in the van, Mother could see the scene that followed clearly. The dogs were unusually large, and they appeared to be part German shepherd. The leader of the pack, who was the size of a large German shepherd, was by no means the largest animal, though he seemed to be the most aggressive. When he saw Christopher, the dog charged him while the others stood close behind.

Although Christopher was well practiced with his rifle, he had never shot a living target. His shooting experience had consisted of firing at tin cans. Yet, now he had only seconds in which to fatally wound this dog or be torn to ribbons by the pack, and he knew that he would be able to get off only one shot. While the enormous white dog raced toward him with fangs bared and saliva flying, Chris raised his rifle to his shoulder and sighted the animal. Then, with the dog nearly upon him, but clearly in his sights, Christopher fired. The bullet went through the dog's chest and into his lungs. The rest of the pack scattered while the wounded animal howled in pain and fled, with Chris chasing him. However, the wound was so severe that he could not run far, and the dog fell dead after a few moments.

Later as Chris explained how he was able to remain calm enough to find the dog in his sights, his explanation sounded very much like that of the three-year-old who had killed the gophers. "I knew that if the dog attacked me the rest of the pack would be on me within seconds," he said simply. "I had time for only one shot, and I had to make that one count."

I have never known Chris to run away from difficulty; he stands his ground to face his problems. A few weeks ago this attitude again surfaced while he was working for his father. After several days of unsuccessful telephone solicitation, he took a few hours off to read a book on sales. He then returned to his duties and was able to set up appointments during his next two phone calls.

I have also learned the importance of patience from Christopher. While I might pronounce a task impossible after only a few moments, Chris is willing to spend hours working on a project. As a small child he was able to catch numerous lizards, toads, and birds because of his patience in tracking the creatures. As an older boy he is loved by all of the children because he is able to remain patient with them. Anyone can talk to him for hours without ever being ignored.

Not long ago he was lying on his back repairing pipes under the kitchen sink while Judah sat between his legs talking a blue streak.

"Let's leave Chris alone for a few minutes," I coaxed the five-year-old to his feet. "He is very busy right now, and I know he is getting tired."

"No," Chris interrupted my efforts, "Let him stay. He's not hurting anything." Delighted, Judah returned to his seat and picked up the conversation in mid-sentence.

From Francesca, who is sixteen, I have learned how to deal with other people. Francesca is so warm and outgoing that she is liked by nearly everyone who meets her. In fact, after she attended her first seminar at BYU, Dr. Rowley took the time to stop me in the hall and tell me that all of Francesca's classmates had been very fond of her. She has the ability to strike up friendly conversations with complete strangers, and she finds common ground with nearly everyone she meets. Her warm smile and personable manner quickly set those around her at ease.

Yet, at the same time she is not intimidated by people who are much older than she, and she is able to stand up for herself. During her Closure seminar at BYU four students in her class, who were in their late thirties and early forties, made a point of disrupting each of the other student's presentations by talking and laughing as loudly as possible, so that the speakers were forced to shout in order to be heard. As the Closure presentation is the culmination of the Degrees by Independent Study program, all of the students are very nervous as they make their presentations, and these four had made the week an especially unpleasant one for the other members of the class.

On the last day of the seminar Francesca was to make her presentation when she saw these four take their places together and prepare to interrupt her talk. "Can you hear us?"

they laughingly called to her as she stood behind the podium arranging her notes.

"Of course," replied Francesca, looking directly at the ill-behaved students. "I haven't heard anyone but you for the past week. Can you hear me?"

They nodded sarcastically. "Good," she continued, "Let me tell you something. You four have managed to disrupt everyone's presentation. Now I am about to give my talk, and I don't want to hear you again until I'm finished. I don't want to hear a murmur or a cough; I want total silence. Is that clear?"

The shocked classmates did not reply, but the room was as quiet as a church for the next hour as Francesca completed her presentation.

From Dominic, who is fourteen, I have learned to appreciate the importance of a good sense of humor. Dominic is wonderfully outgoing, and he is able to find humor in nearly every situation, no matter how solemn. And if something is already silly, Dominic will find a way to make it even sillier. One of his favorite pastimes is parodying popular country western songs, and he has rewritten nearly every really successful western song recorded in the last five years. Under his inspiration, "Lost in the Fifties Tonight," became, "Lost in the Bakery Tonight." "There's a Stranger in my House" was rewritten as, "There's a Head Cold in my House," and "Night by Night," became "Bite by Bite."

His masterpiece, however, is his rendition of "Diggin' up Bones," a popular western song by Randy Travis. For those unfamiliar with the lyrics, the song tells of a jilted husband who is "diggin' up bones" going through his wife's possessions. Each time he finds another of her belongings, he remembers the times they shared together. However, Dominic wondered what would happen if the grief-stricken husband were to take his fascination with his wife's belongings one step further. In his version, the husband comes across a red dress he bought for his wife, and remembering how good she looked in it, he puts it on himself. He is so pleased with the results that he begins to experiment with some of her wigs and makeup:

> I took your long red wig and I stuck it on my head.
> I put on some lipstick -- I was sure to knock 'em dead.
> Then I tried some mascara,
> And some different shades of blushes.
> And I can tell you, darling,
> I know I looked plumb luscious.

By the end of the song, the husband has had a sex change operation and become a "liberated woman."

Because of Dominic's flair for the ridiculous, we hope that he will pursue a career in the field of advertising. When he was about ten years old, he conceived the idea for a Coca-Cola commercial using Quasimodo and Esmeralda. He envisioned using a scene from the movie in which the recently flogged Quasimodo begs the crowd for water. Esmeralda was then to run to him and hand him a Coke. As he drank the cola, Quasimodo was to repeat over and over, "She gave me Coke; she gave me Coke," as he sighs in admiration of her kindness. About two years later a Dr. Pepper commercial appeared using Quasimodo and Esmeralda. The commercial used the same scene which Dominic had suggested, but the dialogue was not nearly as imaginative, and we were disappointed that the advertisers had not known about Dominic's version.

From Victoria, who is thirteen, I have learned the importance of having an enthusiastic attitude and genuinely enjoying life. Since she was a small child, Victoria has had a highly adventurous personality and she has always tried to find ways to make even ordinary occasions more special. On her sixth birthday she wanted to celebrate by riding a horse in the Kentucky Derby. When my parents explained that this would not be possible, she suggested an alternative form of entertainment, a gun fight between her and my father -- with whom she shares a birthday -- using real bullets. To her dismay, this proposal was rejected also, leading her to complain to my parents, "You never let me have any fun."

Today she has found more peaceful ways to celebrate her birthday, but she is still full of adventure. Victoria is a girl who seems to truly find pleasure in even the most ordinary aspects of her life -- whether completing her studies, or playing with Bonaparte, the family dog, or merely enjoying the company of her family. She is able to spread that enthusiasm and pleasure for life to others. She is very generous, and she is not as competitive as some of the other children. When she plays a game, she plays well herself, but she also is gracious with the other players, reminding us that we play for the joy of participating rather than the act of winning. Through her example I have learned that the smallest and most insignificant aspects of life can be the most pleasurable.

From Benjamin, who is eleven, I have learned the importance of sensitivity towards others. Benjamin is one of those rare children who considers how his speech and actions will affect others and places their desires ahead of his own. He is careful not to hurt other people's feelings, and he reminds all of us that we should be more conscientious of those around us. In many ways he has taught us about kindness and gentleness.

From him I have also learned to appreciate laughter. Benji has such an infectious laugh that when he is amused the entire household soon becomes tickled. His vivacious personality keeps all of us entertained and amused.

From Israel, who is nine, I have learned that logic can solve a good many problems. The other children send him to Mother with their petitions because he is able to devise ploys which succeed in getting his wishes fulfilled. Last Fourth of July Mother was not planning to give the school-age children a day off from their studies. Israel made an eloquent plea explaining that "It would be a terrible thing for little children to have to work on the Fourth of July." Mother responded by granting the holiday.

He has used his analytical mind to talk his way out of a few situations with such skill that Mother and I have decided that he really ought to be an attorney. A few years ago he told someone that he thought a certain actress was the most beautiful woman in the world. The child immediately went to Mother with the announcement, and Mother jokingly sent back the message, "I hope she includes you in her will then, because I am cutting you out of mine."

A few moments later Israel appeared to explain that he hated the fact that the actress is more beautiful than Mother. He said that he will be glad when she dies and then Mother will be the most beautiful woman in the world.

Israel was no more than five years old at the time, and it was obvious that he did not really mean any harm to the actress. Rather, he felt that by his compliment to the actress he had put himself in a terrible position and he was trying to talk his way out of it as quickly as possible.

Mother was very shocked by his statement, and she explained to him that she had only been joking about taking him out of her will. "It is certainly alright to think that other people are prettier than Mother," she assured him. She went on to remind him that we would never wish that anyone would die. Israel smiled and looked very pleased -- he would be able to enjoy both of his favorite women without feeling a conflict of loyalty.

From Israel I have also learned the importance of drawing up proper legal documents when doing business with family members. Recently, he, Gabrielle, and Benjamin made plans to build a clubhouse. As the first order of business, Israel drew up a contract stating that the club house, when finished, would belong equally to the three of them, and he insisted that they all sign it. Later, as a result of a disagreement, Benjamin tore up the contract, and Israel went straight to Mother, presented the shredded contract as "evidence," and proceeded to win his "case."

From Gabrielle, who is eight, I have learned the importance of self-confidence and of being sure of one's own abilities. As one girl between two sets of boys, she has learned to insist that others accept her as an equal. Last summer she told Mother that she wanted to enter a one hundred mile foot race and "beat all the men." When asked how she planned to accomplish this feat she replied, "They will stop for water, but I won't. I will keep running and get a head start."

As the eighth child in a large family, Gabrielle could have easily been overlooked much of the time, but she is not a little girl to be ignored. She has a strong personality, and she is very opinionated and extremely vocal. Once a visiting cousin of ours slighted her by telling the other little boys, "Let's don't play with her; she's just a girl," and to this day I don't think she has forgiven him. Yet, she is also very sure of her place in the family.

Gabrielle's birthday is Christmas Day, but unlike some other children who are born on Christmas, she seems to enjoy celebrating her birthday on a worldwide holiday. She once told my mother that she loves sharing a birthday with Jesus and knowing that the entire world celebrates the occasion. She has also said that when she marries she wants the ceremony to take place on Christmas Day, so that her birthday, her wedding anniversary, and Christmas will all be on the same day.

From Stefan, who is six, I have learned to appreciate the importance of individuality. If Stefan wants something, or does not want something, he does not care whether the other members of the family agree -- he goes with his impulse. He is not afraid of teasing or opposition from the other children; he is perfectly certain that he knows what is best for him. In fact, he does not like to think that he is too much like anyone else. Recently Judah was signing one of his compositions and Stefan peeked over his shoulder.

"Why did you put Judah Swann on that composition?" Stefan demanded of his younger brother.

"That's my name," answered Judah as he continued writing.

"Swann is my name," protested a shocked Stefan. "You can't be Swann too."

After a few moments of arguing back and forth they went to Mother to settle the dispute and she explained that they were both named Swann because that was the family name, but that they each had their own first name.

"Well," cried an indignant Stefan, "When I grow up I am not going to be Swann. I am going to be just Stefan." Mother and I did not shatter his hopes by explaining that there are other Stefans in the world also.

Yet, though he sometimes carries his desire for individuality to extremes, Stefan has learned at an early age that it is often good to be unique. He is a boy who proudly marches to the beat of a different drummer.

From Judah, who is five, I have learned the necessity of tenacity and determination. Judah was born without a left hand. His arm is perfectly formed, and he has a left wrist, but he has no hand. He could have allowed the birth defect to seriously hinder his development, but he has refused to be hampered by it. Even as a tiny infant he seemed to sense that his abilities would depend on his dedication -- he could do anything he wanted with a little extra effort.

When the time came for him to begin crawling, he faced his first battle. He began pushing himself up on his hands and knees as babies always do when they are gaining their balance to begin crawling. Though his right hand and arm are perfectly formed, without a left hand his left arm was just enough shorter to prevent him from balancing himself, and every time he attempted to push upward, he immediately fell flat on his face.

It was winter, and the house was chilly. Mother had a one-piece terry cloth suit on him to keep him warm, and she laid him on a blanket on the floor of our den so that he could be near the rest of the family. Everyday from his position on the floor he turned over on his stomach and began his daily workout. Over and over he pushed himself up and fell flat again until his hair and suit were drenched with perspiration, and yet he never cried. At first he could only push half way up before he fell; later he was able to push completely up and to hold the position for just an instant before his arm gave out. Whenever he fell, he merely struggled upwards again and continued the exercise. Mother often walked into the room to see his face red and his tiny muscles tense with exertion, and the sight made her almost ill. Yet, although she wanted to pick him up and tell him not to try, she did not. She would never have encouraged him to crawl, but she knew that it was something that he wanted to do, and she wanted to give him the chance to try.

Whenever she could no longer bear the sight of him silently repeating the exercise, she would turn and leave the room, feeling heartsick, but knowing that what she was doing was ultimately best for him.

He continued for one month, and then one day when he had pushed himself up, he crawled away. He became one of the fastest crawlers in the family, and he moved around the house with incredible ease, crawling on stone floors, and up and down steps without difficulty.

When Judah was a year old, Mother took him to the Carrie Tingley Hospital for Handicapped Children in Albuquerque, New Mexico, so that the doctors could check his development. They found that his motor skills were well developed and that he handled his left arm easily and well. "Don't be worried by the fact that he doesn't crawl," one doctor assured her. "In a few months he will start walking."

"But he does crawl," replied Mother.

"No," countered the doctor, "He scoots or he rolls, but he doesn't crawl. Children with this problem never do."

In order to convince the doctor that Judah did crawl, Mother had to put him on the floor and allow him to demonstrate. Before the day was over, Judah crawled for every doctor he saw.

Since that time he has been equally determined about every aspect of his life. There has been nothing that Judah has not been able to do for himself, and to do beautifully. He even excels at such games as wheel barrow races, where it would appear that he could not even compete. He does not act any differently from the other children, and he does not allow anyone to treat him differently. Once a few years ago Mother had given Stefan two crackers -- "one for each hand." She was about to give Judah one, but he insisted on having two. He held one cracker in his hand, and the other he pressed between his left wrist and his right wrist until he could eat it.

Whatever else Judah may be, he certainly is not "crippled." He is physically beautiful, he is intellectually talented and he is capable of performing the same tasks as the other children. When I look at him, I see his beauty, his wit, and his intelligence; I am never aware of his missing hand. His lack of a hand is never mentioned in our home, it is hardly important enough to notice. So, I feel that perhaps I have learned some of my most important lessons from Judah -- he has taught me and the rest of the family never to allow a disability to become a handicap.

84

A very perceptive friend of ours once remarked that, "You will have only two or three really close friends in your life at one time." I will have many opportunities to meet people, but I will probably be truly good friends with only a handful. Of those friendships, probably only one or two will survive over a long period of time. I have been very fortunate -- I have eleven close friends in my life all the time. There is not one person in my family whom I do not like, or with whom I do not have a good relationship. I think that it would be a terrible shame to have a great many "friends" outside my home but to not be close to the people with whom I live. I am very grateful that my best friends share my last name, and that my happiest memories include my parents and siblings. Perhaps this is one of the great advantages of home-schooling -- it draws families together and creates bonds which last a lifetime.

SIX
"THERE MUST NEEDS BE OPPOSITION. . ."

U ntil I was fourteen years old, I had never experienced adversity. True, Israel's illness had been very serious, but I was too young at the time to really comprehend the fact that my brother might die, and thus the situation did not truly touch me emotionally. As a child and teenager I had basked in the comfort and security of my home, completely unaware that a great storm of opposition was about to shatter our lives.

The days of the trips to spend the day at Dad's office had long since ended. Dad had finally become too busy to listen to my idle chatter; he could no longer spend the fun-filled evenings with us which I had enjoyed during my early childhood. His waking moments were now consumed by his career. Dad now left for work around eight o'clock each morning, and he did not return home until at least nine-thirty or ten o'clock at night. During the time when he was getting the financial institution where he was President-CEO changed to a new computer system, he often worked as late as one o'clock in the morning, and I distinctly recall one instance where he arrived home at four A.M. On that occasion Mother begged him to stay home that day and rest, but he refused, and after approximately three hours sleep, he returned to the office.

These absences were very hard on all of us, but the most

affected were the small children, who were growing up without knowing their father at all. One morning Benjamin, who was then about five, startled Dad by calling after him, "Goodbye, Dad. I'll see you tomorrow!"

"Don't be silly," Dad turned to face him, "You'll see me tonight."

"No," replied Mother, who was standing nearby, "He'll see you tomorrow. He's asleep long before you get home at night."

Benjamin's innocent comment reminded us all of how really far apart we were growing. Dad was never home to have dinner with the family, and he did not eat breakfast with us before he left. Fifteen minutes a day was the most time we were able to spend with him during the week. On weekends, he was exhausted, and he shut himself up in his room while he tried to catch up on a little of the rest which he had missed during the week. Sometimes he had dinner with us on Saturday or Sunday, but many other times he preferred to dine in the solitude of his room.

His overexertion took its toll. My smiling, charming, witty father had been replaced by a tired, ill-tempered being. Friends said that he look as though he had aged ten years, and it was apparent to all that his demanding schedule was wreaking havoc on his health -- he constantly complained of back problems, digestive problems, and insomnia.

Yet, the professional recognition which he had worked so hard to attain was finally his, and because we knew that he deserved the honors and awards, we did our best to be supportive. In 1967, three years before I was born, my father had gone to work for a bankrupt financial institution where, federal authorities had already informed management, the doors were about to close. Dad went to work in the loan department, but within one year he had been promoted to Treasurer/Manager, and the authorities had withdrawn their orders to close the facility.

Under Dad's direction, the financial institution soon became the fastest growing institution of its kind in America, and by 1985 it had $145,000,000 in assets. Dad's accomplishments had not gone unnoticed, and soon federal authorities were asking him to take charge of other bankrupt institutions and merge them with his own. By 1985 he was overseeing branches in Kansas, New Mexico, and Panama as well as the home office in El Paso. He had to visit each of these branches at least once a month, which led to an extensive amount of travel. During

December of 1984 he spent so much time out of town that he laughed to a friend, "I'll only be home for Christmas Day."

In addition to all of this, Dad was a member of several civic organizations, and he was the subject of articles in *USA Today, El Paso Today,* and AT&T's trade magazine. He was riding high to the top of his field, but we feared that he was also racing pellmell toward a heart attack.

Then, one day, it all came to an end. On March 29, 1985, through a set of very bizarre circumstances which still have not been fully explained, my father lost the job which he had held for the past seventeen years. On that afternoon his employers walked into his office and fired him without reason, sending him into a virtual state of shock and throwing our lives into a tailspin. I will never forget the night of March 29, as my father walked through the door of our home carrying his personal possessions from his office -- seventeen years packed into a few cardboard boxes. He was pale, and though he said little, I could see in his face the stress not only of unemployment but of seventeen years of dreams which had been shattered in a few hours. Everything that he had worked for had been taken from him without cause or provocation.

At first, the sheer unfairness of it all struck us as the most shocking element of what had happened. If my father had been unable to fulfill his duties, or if he had shirked his responsibilities in any way, we could at least have understood, but this was not the case. During the last month that Dad held his position, the financial institution grew five million dollars -- an almost unheard of increase in assets for a thirty day period. He was brilliant in his field, and dedicated in his position, and yet he had been dismissed like a common clerk.

The first night I was not able to respond to the news -- it had not had time to sink in. As the next few days passed, however, I began to see the reality of the situation. One day during those early weeks Dad returned to the house after meeting with his attorney. As the family gathered around him to hear the news, he explained to us that his former employers had refused to pay off the last two years of his five-year contract, and they had also refused to pay his accrued leave time. The only funds we would have would be the money he had saved and his pension -- we would have to file a lawsuit to obtain the rest.

When he had finished explaining the situation, the rest of the family withdrew leaving the two of us alone for a moment. "Don't be sad, honey," he gently patted my hand as I fought back the tears which had welled up in my eyes. "Everything will be alright." I looked into his face and saw that he was as near tears as I. For that one emotional moment, I had a glimpse of how he felt. During the next few years I would find that those emotional glimpses would be few and far between -- Dad sensed that he had to be strong for us, and as always, he was our anchor during the storm.

Yet, I was sad, and I was also scared. Years later Dad said of losing his job, "It was like losing an old grandfather who had always taken care of you all of your life and then suddenly died without leaving you any inheritance." My father was forty-eight years old when he lost his job. That blow would be devastating to any man, but unlike most other men his age, Dad's youngest child was one year old while his oldest was fourteen. He had ten young children to feed, clothe, and put through school. I was afraid of losing our home, of going hungry, of being forced out of school. None of these things came to pass -- we never missed a meal or a house payment and we were able to continue with our studies. However, my worst fear was the one which I knew would come to pass -- the fear that our lives would be permanently changed. In one afternoon my carefree, comfortable existence had vanished.

When my father told us that we were filing a law suit, I naively expected to have the whole affair over within a few months. I would quickly learn that haste is not a priority in the legal system. A little less than a year passed before our attorney even filed our suit, and then because of delays in the system, our case did not go immediately to court. In January of 1987 we were told that the case would be coming up, but it was delayed. In March of that year we were told that we would have our date with the judge, only to find that our case had again been delayed. In November of 1988 we received the same news. Finally in March of 1989 the case went to court and we received justice -- the jury ruled unanimously in Dad's favor.

Dad began looking for employment immediately after the loss of his job. We believed that, because of his excellent qualifications, he would be employed again within a few weeks. In this also we would be disappointed. El Paso has few large financial institutions, and most of those are owned by out-of-town holding companies who hire their own executives and send them here. Those banks which were locally owned complained that Dad was too well qualified. He had been making a handsome salary in his former position, and many institutions said that they could not afford to pay him comparably. Everywhere he turned he received the same reply -- in El Paso's already depressed job market, there were no positions for a man of his executive abilities.

It became obvious that we would have to leave the area if Dad were to obtain the kind of position for which he was qualified. But, how could we leave? We had only our savings and Dad's pension, which he had invested. The housing market was as depressed as the job market. It might take us years to sell our large home in the country -- the demand for five bedroom houses several miles from the city was scarce. If we bought a home in another area, we would be forced to make the downpayment with our savings, and to make payments on both houses until we could sell our current home. We were not at all certain that we could afford to do that, and we knew that a home large enough to accommodate our family would be very expensive. The best thing to do seemed to be to stay where we were and see what developed. The risk of moving without already having employment in another area was too great.

The one factor which sustained me and the rest of the family during this time was our faith. If we had not sincerely believed that God would care for us, we would not have been able to continue as we did. Yet, that assurance was always with us, and it gave us the courage to persevere. On many occasions our family gathered to pray about our dwindling finances, and for several months Mother fasted every Tuesday and Thursday. We were certain that regardless of what problems we might have to face, our Father in Heaven was capable of providing all of our needs, and it was to Him that we turned in this time of crisis.

At the same time, however, my parents realized that there would have to be serious budgeting in order for us to survive until Dad could find another job, and this meant reevaluating our priorities. Obviously, they wanted to keep their bills paid, and since they had very few debts this would be possible. They wanted to provide us with the necessities -- food, clothing, shelter, etc. However, they also wanted to keep us in school and to continue us on our accelerated rate of study, and doing this would require a great deal of sacrifice. There had always been sacrifices which had resulted from home-schooling, but it had never been an either/or situation which involved giving up all the little luxuries in order to make our educations possible. Yet now, this was exactly what continuing our educations was to entail.

We could no longer afford to eat out at all -- even hamburgers at McDonalds were totally off limits. Before Dad was fired, Mother and Dad had been in the habit of meeting at an Italian restaurant every Friday night after Dad finished work, and our family had gone to a cafeteria for lunch every Sunday for as long as I could remember. But from the day Dad lost his job both of these activities ceased. Henceforth, we ate all of our meals at home.

Mother cut the grocery bill by buying only necessities. We continued to eat well, but she purchased the week's meals very carefully. During the summertime the fresh plums and nectarines we had always loved were too expensive, and we had to avoid certain dishes which cost too much to prepare. Even so, she wanted us to have some treats, and she splurged by buying candy and colas for Friday evening so that we would have something special at least once a week.

We had to limit our utility bills as much as possible, and this meant that we could not afford to keep our house comfortable during the summer. Although our home is equipped with refrigerated air, the system caused our electric bill to skyrocket, and so we were restricted to using the small evaporative cooler on the breakfast porch of our home. As the El Paso temperatures often soar to well over one hundred degrees in the summmmer months, we sweltered in the heat. However, during the summer of 1985, the temperatures were milder than they had been during some previous years, and for this we were very thankful.

As April dragged on to May and May to June, we grew more and more worried. We were living solely on the money in the bank, and we knew that if Dad did not find employment soon we would have literally eaten up our nest egg. School expenses were also catching up with us. I had finished my Closure Project at BYU and I was ready to graduate, but I had not attended any of my seminars except Foundations. Chris also needed to attend his first seminars.

I am sorry to admit that I was totally unconcerned with anyone's needs except my own. Had I been more mature, and perhaps less spoiled, I would have realized that it was unrealistic to expect them to send us all the way to Provo, Utah, and pay all of our living expenses in addition to the tuitions for the seminars during a year when Dad was unemployed. However, I did not realize this; I had always taken it for granted that they would provide for my education completely, and I fully expected them to do so now. I had completed all of the course work necessary to earn my degree, and it seemed logical to me that I should now be able to complete all of the seminars in one summer and graduate. I was insensitive to the fact that each seminar costs around four hundred dollars. Four hundred dollars times the five seminars multiplies into $2000.00 for my tuitions alone. On top of my school expenses, my parents would have to pay my living expenses for nine weeks in Provo.

Although Mother and Dad explained that they could not possibly meet these demands, they never told me that I was being selfish. In fact, they shared my concern for my school, and they did want me to be able to take at least two seminars in 1985. They also wanted Christopher to attend two seminars. After discussing the situation, they enrolled us in two seminars and rented an apartment in Provo for the month of July. My three remaining seminars would have to wait until the following year, but I was grateful to be attending at least two.

Thus, in spite of our problems I was fairly happy during the first part of June, and I counted off the days unti I would leave for Provo. Then, on June 15, my parents' twenty-second wedding anniversary, my brother walked outside early in the morning and discovered that our pick-up truck had been stolen! In my father's former position he had been furnished with a station wagon which was a little too small for our family but which provided adequate transportation. Of course, after he was fired we had to return the vehicle and our pick-up truck had been our only source of transportation. Now, it too was gone, and we were stranded.

It was Saturday and Dad and the boys needed to drive to our farm to feed his thoroughbred horses. Therefore, we were desperate for a vehicle. We called the police, but the officer who made out the report told us that there was no chance of recovering our truck -- it had, no doubt, already been taken across the Mexican border. We could not afford to buy any sort of a car or truck because of our desperate financial situation.

My parents had some friends who had an old Pinto, and though the vehicle was hardly in running condition, they graciously insisted on loaning it to us until we could afford to purchase a car. Harry picked Dad up and drove him to our farm, while we went to the house to see our "new car." We were sitting and talking with Barbara in the living room when Dad and Harry returned. By now we were so accustomed to hearing bad news that we expeced it, but when we saw the look on Dad's face we knew that something was wrong.

Disconsolate, he fell onto the couch and in an angry, frustrated, but quiet tone he told us that when he and Harry arrived at our farm they had found that one of our most beautiful new foals had been shot and then torn to pieces by wild dogs. The shooting was obviously deliberate, for the colt had been taken from his mother before being killed. The needless cruelty of the act horrified us; no one could have benefited in any way from murdering a young animal in such a fashion. The event was made all the more grotesque by the fact that it occurred on the same day that the truck was stolen and that both had happened on my parents' wedding anniversary. We could not help wondering why we had been singled out for such relentless persecution.

Two weeks later Dad, Christopher, and I left to go to Provo, Utah, for a month. Mother and Dad had arranged for us to have a chaperone, and the chaperone had asked Dad to drive her Volkswagen van to Provo while she flew. The arrangement worked out well since Mother would need the Pinto here while we were gone. In spite of our difficulties, Dad was in unusually good spirits on that trip. During the length of the two day trip, he sang and talked to us as though we did not have a care in the world. Part of the reason for his excitement lay in the fact that as soon as he had gotten us settled in our apartment he would fly from Salt Lake City to San Francisco, California, where a Canadian businessmen had asked him to consult on the purchase of several cruise ships. Dad was paying his own expenses, but his check for his consulting services would provide us with a little income again.

We arrived in Provo on Sunday and Dad turned us over to the care of our chaperone. We then spent the evening together, and he stayed the night with us. The following morning he rose early and we kissed him goodbye before he left for the Salt Lake City airport. There was so much enthusiasm in his face as he said goodbye, and I hoped that this consulting job would turn into a permanent situation.

When I returned home a month later I learned that although he had gone to California and done a considerable amount of work, he had not been paid for his services. This was one of the difficult lessons we would learn about Dad's new line of work -- there is no collection agency for financial consultants. Although many of the businessmen were honest, Dad also worked for several people who never paid his fee or even covered his expenses. Every time that he went out on another job, we lost money if his client did not give him a check. During the month of September, he spent five thousand dollars of his own money traveling to Santa Fe, New Mexico, to consult for a bankrupt savings and loan. Though he made considerable strides in alleviating the condition of the institution, he was never paid for any of his work.

As we labored on through the summer and the early fall, we grew less and less certain of what was going to happen to us.

94

We knew that our savings were disappearing quickly -- my parents had spent approximately three thousand dollars sending us to our seminars, and Dad had spent a great deal of his own money performing unrewarded tasks. We did not have the funds for even desperately needed possessions, such as a new car.

We had nicknamed the Pinto "the Mercedes" because it was the antithesis of a luxury car. The dashboard was cracked, the upholstery was coming out of the seats and the frame was dented. Yet, it's internal problems far surpassed it's cosmetic defects. The owner was constantly tinkering with it in an effort to fix all of the problems, but even so it could hardly be driven. My brothers had to push it to get it started, and then it had no acceleration. It was not capable of climbing even the smallest incline, and the engine stalled habitually.

I am ashamed to confess that when I was a little girl, I made terrible fun of people who drove old, dilapidated cars. Mother, who had ridden in a good many old cars as a child, reprimanded me for my thoughtlessness by saying, "No one likes to drive old, rundown cars, Alexandra. If they could afford to have a nicer car, they would." I was not convinced; I somehow believed that if people were simply willing to spend a little more money they could live better. Now, when I was fourteen, my words came back to haunt me, and I learned a lesson in compassion from our trials with the Pinto.

One day Mother and I were in a shopping center, and she prepared to pull out of the parking lot. The principal exit was a very small incline which no ordinary vehicle would have difficulty climbing. However, as Mother attempted to drive up the hill, the Pinto stalled. She pushed the accelerator completely down, only to find us rolling backward toward the cars behind us. Immediately she braked, and then tried to accelerate again, with the same result. In the meantime, about five cars had lined up behind us, and irritation was apparent in the faces of the other drivers. In my mind I could hear them making the very comments I would have made only a few months before had I been they.

Finally, Mother realized that we were not going to be able to force the Pinto up the hill, and she instructed me to get out of the car and ask each driver behind us to pass our vehicle. With disgusted looks, they complied, and then she allowed the Pinto to roll backwards until we were again on level ground. She turned the car around and drove out the backstreet exit.

She had been silent as we left the parking lot and made our way onto the freeway, but now she burst into tears. "I hate those people!" she sobbed, referring to Dad's former employers. "I hate them! I hate what they've done to us!" I did not know how to respond. Gently I put my arm around her, knowing that this was embarrassment and frustration speaking rather than Mother. In a moment she had regained her composure and apologized for the outburst.

As for me, I was able to sympathize with Mother's feelings, but I, myself, was nowhere near tears. Instead, a realization had come to me that Mother's speeches about compassion had never been able to produce. I had learned a very important lesson that day, and I would never again be tempted to sneer at anyone driving an old car.

Fall came and the holidays approached. Ordinarily, this was my favorite time of year, but this year the mood was less than celebratory. However, before Thanksgiving two events took place which brightened everyone's spirits considerably. First, we were able to replace the Pinto. The woman who had acted as our chaperone for school that year decided to sell her fourteen-year-old Volkswagen van. Though the van was designed for only seven passengers, with a little crowding we could squeeze in the entire family. Further, it seemed to be in better condition than the Pinto and the price was within our budget. My parents bought it and returned "the Mercedes" to Harry and Barbara with happy hearts. After three months of riding in the Pinto, the first time we drove to the grocery store in our van, I felt as though I were riding in a Rolls Royce.

The second event which brightened the holidays for us was a job offer from a large corporation in Houston with holdings in El Paso. They were interested in hiring Dad as a financial consultant to oversee some of their properties here. After nearly nine months of unemployment, we were so delighted with the prospect that we were nearly able to forget all of our previous troubles.

That Thanksgiving was a happy one as we sat around our table thanking God for His kindness. I reflected on all that had happened to us in the past year, and I realized that we really had been very blessed that the damage had not been worse. We had spent all of our savings, but we still had Dad's pension. We children had not really done without much -- though we had been limited in our expenditures we had each received birthday presents and there would most certainly be something under the tree for each of us at Christmas. We were all together. In spite of the fact that we had been without health insurance for nine months, no one in the family had been sick or hurt. We had kept our bills paid, and we children had been able to continue with our studies. I had even begun my master's degree program in the September semester. We realized that, in spite of our losses, we had much to be grateful for. And when the time came for each of us to count our blessings, Benjamin expressed a sentiment which was in all of our hearts. "I'm thankful," he said sweetly, "that I just have this feeling that Dad has a job."

Dad did have a job, and on December 15 he began working. He was being paid at half his previous salary, and he was not working in his field of banking, but the fact that he was working at all was a cause for celebration. Despite our setbacks, Christmas of 1985 stands out in my mind as the happiest I can remember. It was not one of our more lavish holidays, for the spending for each person had been severely limited, but there was a spirit of joy and peace in our household which I had not felt for a long time. As I watched my father on Christmas Eve, eating the candies which Judah ran back and forth bringing to him, I knew that I had received a gift far more precious than any amount of money could buy. I had my father back. Every trace of the nervous, driven man had disappeared; Dad no longer complained of the health problems which had plagued him the year before. As our family celebrated the birth of the Prince of Peace, I rejoiced at the peace which had once again filled my family. I knew that the harmony which we had rediscovered would always be ours, and that the head of our household would be near to share our lives.

In January we began to organize our new schedules. Dad leased a T-Bird to take to work, while we had the van to use for grocery shopping and taking the boys to the farm. Dad was home every evening now, and we enjoyed the time we spent together. His paycheck had relieved the immediate financial burden of having to withdraw money from the bank to live on. He had invested his pension in the stock market, and he was making excellent dividends. It looked as though our financial position would soon resolve itself.

However, we quickly found that our monetary worries were by no means over. Dad's salary gave us just enough to buy groceries and pay household bills and school expenses, with no extras. The frugal budget we had accustomed ourselves to while he was unemployed continued, and it brought many changes in our lifestyle which I had not expected. Before this Mother and Dad had always spent a great deal of money on clothes for us; now she bought blue jeans and tennis shoes. When I graduated from BYU, my aunt sent me five hundred dollars; by saving carefully, I could buy my own clothes for the next two years, but this helped only marginally. Boxes of clothes from friends and from my aunt were put to good use -- we did not throw anything away that we could possibly use. Mother and Dad were stricter with themselves in this area than they were with us -- they received presents and made purchases for themselves only at their birthdays and Christmas. During the rest of the year they did not spend any money on themselves.

Our house suffered as well. With ten children living in any home the need for repairs is constant -- if for no other reason simply because everything receives so much greater wear than that for which it was designed. Now, however, if something broke, it stayed broken. We lived for almost a year without a working faucet on the kitchen sink because we could not afford to have it replaced. We could not afford the desperately needed paint job for the house, and we could not afford to replace the sheers which hung in tatters on the living room window. As the years passed more and more items in our house needed repair or replacement. Our bath towels were as thin as tissue paper because we could not afford new linens. We could not buy new glassware or china; thus, we drank from plastic glasses.

The limiations on utility bills were still in force, and we sweltered during the summer and shivered during the winter because we could not afford to run the heat and air conditioning. Mother would turn on the heat when she got up each morning and allow it to run for a couple of hours to take the chill off the house. Then she would turn it off until the following morning. Fortunately, the winters in El Paso are mild, and by dressing warmly we were able to survive without too much discomfort. I actually think we were less uncomfortable during the winter months than we were in summer.

Still, for all the problems, it seemed that the next two years were a calm in the storm. Our family spent wonderful times together. Mother and Dad wanted us to continue to have special moments, and they found ways to arrange for us to have little holidays which would not be expensive.

On summer weekends we spent many Saturday and Sunday evenings at our farm. Dad organized us into teams, and we ran relay races. We then finished many pleasant afternoons by going on long walks together. On other days, Mother prepared picnics for us to take there. At our house, a picnic means plenty of fried chicken, biscuits, potato salad, deviled eggs, chips, dips and cheese ball with crackers, as well as several six packs of soft drinks. When the weather was pleasant, we ate a leisurely meal and then spent the rest of the afternoon enjoying the remaining soft drinks in the sunshine. These inexpensive outings with the family were just as enjoyable as the times we had previously spent together in costly entertainment.

Thus, although we did not have many material luxuries, we enjoyed happy moments together. Then, in March of 1987 we received news that the corporation for which Dad worked wanted him to come to Houston to take over some of their interests in their headquarters. Unfortunately, the move carried with it no increase in salary. Dad had ninety days to set his affairs in order before leaving in mid-July.

The news came at a very bad time. Our house was in need of numerous repairs before it could even be listed with a real estate agent. Further, we were barely bringing in enough income to keep our school expenses and bills paid. We were in less of a position to leave the El Paso area than we had been after Dad lost his job, for we no longer had any savings except Dad's pension plan, and we did not want to tap into that. We were not at all certain that we could afford a home large enough to accommodate our family. Our only consolation was that because of the oil crisis the Houston housing market was very depressed, and we hoped that we could find a large home which had been greatly reduced in price.

The ninety days passed very quickly, and when July came we were no closer to being ready to leave than we had been in March. Mother and Dad decided that he would spend his weekends looking for an affordable home there before we listed our current residence with a realtor. As the day for his departure approached, our family became increasingly depressed. Throughout all of our problems during the past two years, we had been able to stay together. Now Dad was leaving for an indefinite period of time, and it seemed as though even the pleasure we had derived from our family was being taken away from us.

On the Fourth of July that year, knowing that he would be leaving in a week and unsure of when we would see each other again, Dad decided that he would drive the family to Silver City, New Mexico, a mountain resort near a beautiful State Park with pine forests and lakes. Mother packed a picnic and we rose early on Saturday morning to make the trip. After eating our lunch in the state park, we went for a hike through the woods. Some of the small children had never seen so many trees at once, and being accustomed to the desert scenery at home, they were particularly excited by the greenery surrounding them. Even I, who have been in forests on a number of occasions, felt a childish delight to find myself amid acres and acres of sweet-smelling pine. And yet, though at any other time I would have had a wonderful day, the beauty of the park could not obliterate the sadness I felt knowing that we had only a week left together. The following Saturday Dad packed his car and said goodbye to the family. I had promised myself that I would not cry, but in the end I found myself sobbing on his shoulder as I kissed him. He put his arms around me and promised that he would find a house in Houston and that we would be joining him quickly. Then he kissed Mother and the other children and took the last of his bags to his car. We stood in the front yard waving as he drove off.

That month passed very slowly for all of us. We kept in touch with Dad by making a cassette tape for him every weekend. All day Saturday and Sunday the tape recorder was in service as each member of the family took the time to record a short message for Dad. He made tapes for us also, and we searched through the mail eagerly looking for his messages. When a tape did arrive, listening to it was the high point of our evening. All of us would gather around the dining table or in the living room to hear the sound of our father's voice and find out what he had been doing since he had been away. He also called Mother several times during the first month, but the expense of the telephone bill precluded his doing this too often.

August 8 is Dominic's birthday, and as the time approached I could see Dominic becoming more and more downcast because his father would not be home to celebrate. Mother bought him his birthday present and took him to lunch -- now that Dad was again employed we had been able to reinstate birthday lunches as one time of the year when eating out was acceptable. Still, though he was pleased with his present, he could not become cheerful about his birthday. "Dad will call," Mother promised, noting how disheartened he seemed.

About three days before Dominic's birthday Mother announced that a family friend was coming for a visit. "At least, even though Daddy won't be here, you can celebrate with her instead," she encouraged Dominic. Mother played up the approaching visit from our friend, reminding us of how much fun it would be to have her here, and what a pleasant time we would spend together.

August 8 fell on a Saturday that year, and on Friday evening Mother took Francesca and me and drove to the airport to pick up our friend. On the way I thought of the many times that Mother and I had driven there to pick up Dad coming in from one of his trips. It was almost a tradition -- ever since the other children had been old enough to leave alone I had gone with her to the airport whenever she picked up Dad. It seemed very strange to think that tonight he would not be there.

We entered the airport and waited for our friend's flight. When the flight arrived, we walked upstairs and watched the passengers entering the airport. Our friend is about five feet tall, and my eyes searched the crowd for a tiny middle-aged woman. The stream of passengers continued until it looked as though the plane was almost empty, and still there was no sign of her. "I hope she didn't miss her flight," Mother looked concerned.

Suddenly, I saw Dad stepping from the hallway into the airport. I was so shocked that at first I could not believe it was he. Then a dozen ridiculous questions rushed through my mind: What was he doing here? Had Mother known he was coming? How did he book the same flight as Karen? Then, all at once, the truth of the matter hit me and I burst out laughing. Usually I can tell when Mother is playing a joke on us, but this time I never even suspected. And of all the jokes she has ever played, I enjoyed that one the most.

Dad's sister, with whom he was staying in Houston, had given him the money to fly home for Dominic's birthday. I have enjoyed few weekends as much as that one. Having Dad home again after his absence caused me to realize how much I had missed him. I was so delighted that I could do nothing but thank the Lord that He had allowed him to come home, even if for only a weekend.

The news which Dad brought from Houston was not good, however. He had looked at a number of homes, and even though the prices of housing were greatly reduced, we still could not afford a residence there. Dad was sending half his paycheck home, and keeping half there to live on. The result was that neither of us had any money. However, we knew from previous experience that it would be unwise to risk more unemployment by having him quit his job to come home. We would just have to suffer through, hoping that either he would receive a pay raise, we would eventually find an affordable home, or both.

On Sunday afternoon he left to return to Houston, leaving us more uncertain than ever of how much longer this forced separation would last. We went through August and early September, and Dad called Stefan on his birthday. On Labor Day, my aunt paid Dad's way home for the weekend, and we were able to spend some very pleasant time together. Then of course, he was back in Houston again.

"Before Dad lost his job we had plenty of money but we were never together," I complained to Mother one day. "Now he doesn't even live here and we don't have the money either." We were all plagued by the distinct feeling that we were being short-changed. It looked as if this arrangement might last for several years, and I did not think that I could stand for us to be apart that long. Mother began praying diligently that Dad would be able to come home.

The last week of September, Dad called to say that the corporation was sending him back to El Paso to supervise one of their projects, and that he would be here through the holidays. It was an answer to prayer, and we were ecstatic. He arrived home on October 1, and we knew that this time he would not be leaving in two days to return to Houston.

As happy as we were to have Dad home through Christmas, we should have known that there would be at least one catastrophe to dampen our spirits. Dad had almost doubled his pension through his investments in the stock market, and at the rate that his money was increasing we would soon have a considerable savings. Then, like millions of other Americans, we became the victims of "Black Monday," and we lost nearly all of the profits he had made through his investment, although the principal sum was still in tact. After the crash, the wavering of the market took our stocks up a few points one day, and erased all our gains the next. The only positive aspect of the situation was that at least Dad was employed and we could leave the funds alone until the market began to climb again.

Still, we enjoyed a wonderful Thanksgiving and Christmas, and to counter the tragedy in the market an exciting new development took place during those three months while Dad was home. A man who had been a friend of his for many years contacted him with what seemed to be an excellent opportunity. The man was working with another gentlemen who had been placed in charge of a Swedish pension plan which he was to invest in the United States. Because of Dad's brilliant reputation and financial expertise they wanted him to act as the consultant for a generous salary.

I had not seen Dad so enthused in years. Finance was his speciality, and particularly international finance. This job was everything which he had hoped for.

The two men decided to buy an international bank in the Caribbean and to hire Dad as the President of the institution. Dad made all of the arrangements and purchased the bank charter for them. By January he had taken care of all the details.

His Houston employer was now ready for him to return to Houston to assume his duties there. Although Dad did not want to leave at this time, he did not want to risk quitting his present job before his new position was firm, and he returned to Houston.

He had been there two weeks when his friend called to say that they were ready to go to the Caribbean and open the facility. They needed Dad there as quickly as possible. This was the time for him to quit his job and embark on his new career. Resolutely, he took the step. His employers asked him to take a leave of absence rather than quitting, but Dad knew that this project would require his undivided attention, and he resigned his post. Two days later he was on his way to the Caribbean.

Two weeks later he was home again. He had been in the Caribbean only a few days when the two bank owners had become embroiled in a terrible dispute. One of the owners had decided to cut the other out. A lawsuit was filed and the bank was never opened. Dad, of course, was once again unemployed.

With a dwindling pension, no savings and no income, we were financially in worse straits than we had ever been. Yet, we had been disappointed so many times in the past three years that this time his unemployment did not have the same impact. In spite of the fact that we had no income, I was glad that he was home to stay.

We examined our options; we knew that we could rule out moving to another area along with his finding a suitable position here. The only thing that remained was for us to go into business for ourselves.

Thus, at the age of fifty-one, Dad was forced to start over again in a completely new career field. He did not allow either the difficulty of the process or his Irish pride to stand in his way, but immediately began his new career. He went to school to get an insurance license, and after several months he became an independent agent. Another nine months of unemployment and living solely on his pension passed before he began to draw income again, and then his salary came from consulting. However, he now owns his own insurance agency and he continues to operate his consulting firm. For the first time in nearly four years, our future looks bright.

On one of my more recent travels to BYU I had the honor of meeting Ezra Taft Benson, President of the LDS Church, and his son Dr. Reed Benson, who teaches Book of Mormon at BYU. During one of our conversations, Dr. Benson made the statement, "There must needs be opposition in all things." I had never heard that before, but from the moment Dr. Benson said it, I knew that it was true, and that statement helped me to put into perspective all of the traumas my family has met with during the past four years.

My parents had taught me that Satan loves adversity and that when something tragic happens, it is because something wonderful will follow and the Adversary is angry. The more I thought about that philosophy the more I liked and agreed with it. The opposition with which we have met has not been to no avail; there has been much that has been accomplished because of it. I have learned many lessons from our travails which would otherwise have eluded me. Opposition is a necessary part of life; there can be no escaping it. It is how we face opposition that determines how well we survive it.

In this my parents have set a wonderful example for us. My father is like a strong stone wall built on a heavy foundation. In the same way that a stone wall survives numerous storms, buffetings from the winds, and the erosion of water and weather, my father has survived a good many tribulations.

When I was in grade school I read a story entitled "The Gift of Going Without." The author had grown up in a home where there was neither electricity nor running water. She told of having to heat an iron on the stove before she could press her clothes, of having to pump water and then boil it for her bath, and of using an old-fashioned icebox. She then told how as an adult she remembered the old-fashioned pump everytime she turned on the kitchen faucet, and recalled the old icebox whenever she opened her refrigerator.

At the time that I read the story, I did not understand it, and I can recall skeptically telling Mother that I did not see how going without could possibly be a gift. Now, I too, possess the gift. The "gift" of which she spoke was not "going without" but what she learned from those sacrifices. I, too, have learned a great deal from my family's experiences. I have gained a new compassion and insight, and I have learned that happiness is not bound up in expensive restaurants or expensive clothes or nice cars. While all of those items are wonderful, and I would like to possess them as much as anyone, I have found that I can be just as happy without them, and that is a nice realization. Most of all, however, my family's sacrifices have made me grateful for what we do have. My parents have been willing to give up many material comforts to insure that we will have our educations, as well as the necessities of food and shelter, and this has meant a great deal to me. Whenever I recall the fact that my parents chose to teach me at home, I will always remember that they did so under the most difficult of circumstances. Our educations were their gift to us during the time that Dad was unemployed, and during the years when he worked for a meager income. Because I know of the love and dedication which went into that gift, I now value my education not only in terms of what it means to me, but also in terms of what it cost my parents to obtain it for me.

SEVEN
FINISHING THE RACE

The large, well-lighted room was humming with the sounds of supressed laughter and quiet conversation among the members of the DIS program's 1986 graduating class. Outside, the beautifully manicured campus grounds were buzzing with activity as students hurried to and from classes on this warm, slightly muggy August afternoon. However, most seemed oblivious to the heat, for they appeared to be concentrating on more important matters.

Inside the air-conditioned building, seated at a table next to Mother, I was thinking neither of the students outside, nor of those conversing around me. My thoughts were focused on the small blue folder in front of me, containing the notes for the hour-long presentation I was about to make. This was the long awaited Closure week at BYU, and this presentation was the culmination of my work at the university – the last event before my graduation. Fifteen years old, I would be the youngest student to graduate from BYU in its 111 year history.

That morning I had met Dr. Frank Santiago, with whom Mother had spoken at the time of my enrollment, and he had inquired about my presentation, entitled "Humanism -- America's State Religion?" However, as I waited to be introduced, I was literally stunned to see three strangers from the university's administration enter the room with Dr. Santiago and take their seats. Also present were a member of the university's press office who had conducted a two-hour interview with me that morning and Dr. Rawson, the director of the Degrees by Independent Study Program.

I had rehearsed my talk every day for three and a half weeks. I knew my material thoroughly, but I feared that when I started to speak, my mind would become a blank and I would make a complete fool of myself. As the time approached for the first presentation to conclude and mine to begin, my heart beat ever faster until I could hardly catch my breath.

At last the moment arrived. My chest felt tight and my hands were slightly clammy, as at the sound of my name, I stood and walked slowly to the podium. In the back of the room, Mother was passing around the folders containing additional information and visual aids which I had prepared to help my audience follow the presentation more easily. "How appropriate that she should be here," I thought to myself. She had been present when I attended my first seminar, and it seemed only proper that she should be with me as I attended my final seminar.

Upon seeing that all the folders had been passed around, I began to speak. As my voice rose clearly over the auditorium, my fear suddenly vanished, silence enveloped the room, and I could see that I held a captive audience. For one hour I impressed upon my listeners the dangers of Humanism in the courts, schools, and political arenas of America. Even Dr. Rawson, who had slipped in and out of the room during the course of the day, remained motionless. As I spoke, I felt a sense of triumph surging through me, for I realized that the last three years of my life -- the three years I had spent at BYU -- had climaxed in that hour. All of the hard work had been worthwhile.

As I returned to my seat amid the congratulations of both students and faculty, Mother's warm smile assured me that the presentation had been a success. Both classmates and faculty members were extremely receptive with nearly everyone taking part in the fifteen minute question and answer session I had scheduled at the end of the presentation, and I had several requests for copies of the original project. With a great sense of relief I listened to the other presentations that afternoon, and as I sat there I allowed myself to reflect upon the events which had brought me to that moment.

I had begun to work on my Closure Project the year before, in the spring of 1985. By then I had completed nearly all of the course work necessary to earn my bachelor's degree. All I lacked were five seminars and a final project. One of the graduation requirements of the DIS program is that each student write a fifty to seventy-five page Closure Project, the equivalent of a bachelor's thesis. The project, in its written form, is bound and becomes a permanent part of the university's library, but it must also be presented in oral form at the university during Closure Week. Consequently, it must be well documented, well written, and typed according to certain stylistic requirements.

Mother and I had spent several months discussing possible topics, and we finally decided upon "Humanism -- America's State Religion?" as my subject. A few years before, an El Paso woman who had spent eighteen years researching the subject of Humanism had appeared on a local television program. Amazingly, Mother remembered her name. When the time came for me to begin researching my topic, I contacted her and she agreed to allow me to use her library for my research. Dad drove me to her house on his way to work on a couple of mornings, and I spent the days gathering material for my project. She also allowed me to take books home. When I had compiled all of my notes, I started writing, and within six weeks, I had turned out the first typed draft of my paper and submitted it to the school.

BYU assigned as my mentor Dr. Chauncey Riddle, who is considered one of the nation's foremost authorities on the subject of Humanism. After reviewing my paper, Dr. Riddle returned it for minor revisions in content and major revisions in form. I altered the thesis to conform to his suggestions, and then Mother, Dad, and I worked retyping it. We had only a portable electric typewriter on which to work, and typing was, thus, slow and laborious. Fortunately, both of my parents type extremely well, and they did the bulk of the work. Once again we submitted my paper, and once again Dr. Riddle asked for minor changes in the paper's content. I was able to make the corrections in the text very quickly, but, of course, the entire paper had to be retyped. Again my parents helped, but this time I did most of the typing. I spent many beautiful summer evenings on the breakfast porch of our house, as I typed the final draft of my paper. When I was finally finished I crossed my fingers and mailed it back to the school. This time, Dr. Riddle found it satisfactory and accepted it.

In its final draft my Closure Project was forty-eight pages long and contained 118 footnotes. Divided into five sections of about ten pages each, the paper examined three areas in which Humanism has infiltrated American life: the courts, the classroom, and the political arena. It also contained a detailed explanation of the Humanist Manifestoes I and II, and it concluded with a discussion of Humanism and the constitution of the United States. I was very pleased with the project, but I was also a little surprised by the interest the paper generated. In each of my seminars where I happened to discuss the paper with my classmates, invariably three or four of them asked for copies. During one break when I was discussing the paper with some of the other students, one of my professors overheard and offered to pay for a copy if I would xerox one for him. Almost without exception, it received a very positive response on campus.

I was glad that my project had earned the acceptance of my fellow students and instructors, because, for me, total acceptance at BYU was important. I loved my school, and I wanted my school to love me. Although I seldom had cause to feel discriminated against at BYU, there were times when I imagined that a professor was critical of my age. When I attended the Man and the Universe seminar, we were required to visit a state training hospital for the mentally retarded. Fourteen years old, I had never been inside a mental institution and was not prepared for the shrieks which resounded throughout the building, nor for the tears of the wailing phenylketonuria patient who was led out so that we could see the value of the invention of PKU tests, nor for the grotesque physical deformities which greeted my eyes. As my stomach churned, I sincerely hoped that I would not have to ask to be excused. When the room began to spin slowly, however, I realized that I would either have to be embarrassed by asking to be excused or by fainting. I quietly asked the professor for permission to leave and quickly walked out of the building and sat down on the grass where the warm summer air revived me. The following day, as we hiked through a Utah canyon, the professor turned to me and remarked that he "didn't know the Yellow Rose of Texas was a wimp."

Later, in the course of a conversation with Christopher, who was then thirteen, I learned that several of the other young women had turned very pale during the tour, and that one of the middle-aged men -- who was apparently searching for a means to leave the building without also appearing to be a "wimp" -- repeatedly asked Christopher how he felt, assuring him that he would be happy to take him outside, should my brother become ill. I was relieved when later I heard other students complaining that this same professor had made rude remarks to them. At least, I realized that his attitude reflected his own personality rather than some prejudice against me.

Fortunately, to the large majority of the professors it seemed to make no difference either that we were younger than ordinary university students or that we were Baptists. One of these was the English professor, Don Norton. He was a man who seemed always to be genuinely concerned about truly teaching and helping his students rather than just showing them how much more knowledge he had than they. Norton always treated my siblings and me with respect and consideration, never trying to make us feel like outsiders.

A second professor who displayed no bias was Dr. John Halliday, the music professor. Although he was teaching a very complicated subject to a group of novices, he exercised excellent judgment in dealing with his student's mistakes. In my opinion he was a tremendous asset to the faculty, and I was very sorry to learn of his recent death.

Another exceptional instructor was Dr. Walter Bowen, who taught in the university's theology department. He treated us with a kindness and respect which was deeply appreciated. In fact, he went out of his way to make us feel as though we belonged by personally introducing us to many of the seminar's guest speakers. Sensing that we were probably very homesick after being away from our family for several weeks, he and his wife were even kind enough to take us on a picnic in the Provo Canyon. He picked us up after class and drove us by his house where Mrs. Bowen was waiting for us with a delicious meal packed and ready to go. We spent a pleasant evening chatting with the two of them in the cool mountain air. The picnic was one of the high points of the seminar, and the time spent with the Bowen's helped us not to feel so lonely.

Of course, the great majority of my professors were neither unusually friendly nor unusually hostile. However, the fact remained that we were children in a program designed for adults, and we had to work very hard to maintain our status. Fortunately, we were accustomed to applying ourselves, for Mother had never accepted second best from us, and she had taught us not to accept it from ourselves. As far as she was concerned, a professor's attitude had nothing to do with our performance in a course, and, in fact, if we sensed that an instructor disliked us, she made us work harder. Therefore, regardless of whatever personal conflicts we might face at BYU, we always earned top grades.

Under the best of circumstances there are many irritating aspects of being a teenager in college which one does not consider until confronted with the situation. When I was in college I was too young to drive, and, therefore, I had to rely on adults to drive me to any sites that my assignments might require I visit. In Man and Beauty I was required to visit various arts and crafts shows, as well as different art galleries. Mother, who went into labor on the day that I was scheduled to visit one show was simply unable to take me and arranged for a friend of hers to pick me up on two different afternoons and take me to see the shows. Two weeks later, when I was required to interview two of the artists whose work I had seen in my tour of art galleries, this same friend offered to take me to my destination. However, these were the only two occasions on which Mother ever pressed one of her friends into service. Usually she made time in her schedule to take me to my required destinations.

One assignment required that I compose a photo essay of my community. During the lunch hour on different days Mother drove me around the area so that I could photograph the more interesting sites -- a project which took several days to complete.

Being unable to drive also meant that I was unable to pick up books from the library. At BYU this really was not a problem, for I seldom needed extra material in order to complete an assignment, but when I progressed on to graduate work, where I might need to check out as many as five different books for one assignment, my lack of transportation became more irritating. Fortunately, Dad was always willing to lend a hand. I would call the library and request that the books I needed be put aside and then in the morning before he left for work I would give him a list of books he would be picking up. At night on his way home he would stop and get them for me, and when I finished he would take them back. During some semesters he had to do this as often as two or three times, but he never complained.

However, I encountered the most frustrating aspects of my unusual situation while attending seminars at BYU. Of course, my brother and I were too young to travel alone. During 1985 when my father was first unemployed, Chris and I spent four weeks in Provo with our chaperone. We found that her presence was actually rather nice, for Chris and I had to spend much of our time either attending lectures or studying, and our chaperone was there to cook and keep the apartment for us. In addition, she had brought her car, and whenever we were pressed for time or had to attend classes in the evening, she was able to drive us.

The following year, though, when Christopher and Francesca and I returned to finish our seminars, I found myself confronted with a series of annoying little mishaps, most of which were caused by my chaperone. The same woman who had filled in the year before insisted on accompanying us again. My parents knew that in the intervening year she had experienced problems with her leg and that she had been to see a number of doctors. Though they were prepared to find someone else to act as chaperone, she insisted that she was physically fit and that she wanted to make the second trip.

Upon arrival, however, she began to behave in a very erratic manner. She immediately decided that our apartment was totally unsuitable because it was located on the second floor of the building. (Although she claimed that because of the problems she had experienced with her leg she was unable to climb stairs, she spent most of the day every day nimbly running up and down the long flight.) While my father, who had driven us to Provo and spent the night to get us settled, was present, she did not say too much on this subject, but the moment he left she began to demand that we move to another apartment across town. As my parents had already paid one month's rent on our current apartment, I really could not justify meeting such unrealistic demands. In protest, she camped out in our living room and slept in her car.

I had other problems as well. The traveler's checks which my father had purchased for the trip had been drawn up improperly and could not be cashed. We were left nine hundred miles from home with only the forty dollars Dad had given us before he left. Although this was the type of problem for which one has a chaperone, mine was too busy trying to persuade us to find new quarters to be of assistance. Panic stricken, I spent the next twenty-four hours desperately trying to rectify the situation. Finally, I called the American Express office in Salt Lake City and asked if the checks could simply be reissued. Even then, the representative asked if I had a driver's license to show the teller who would be reissuing my checks, but upon learning that I was only fifteen, she considerately arranged to have all of the checks replaced.

I felt rather victorious at having been able to resolve a difficult situation with little help. Unfortunately, our chaperone did not share my jubilation. She was now upset because she had not only been placed in an upstairs apartment, but the traveler's checks had been issued in my name rather than hers.

In addition, Mother had told us to have Christopher's shirts professionally laundered while our traveling companion felt they should be handwashed. This time she protested by throwing a temper tantrum as she drove us to the drycleaners.

Fortunately, soon after this the Reign of Terror ended -- midway through the trip she called her husband and asked him to take her home. Before they left, she cooked a few last meals in which they ate most of our groceries, and then they were on their way. Even though we had been abandoned, we were better off without her.

In spite of these minor irritations, however, we managed to survive BYU. By the summer of 1985, I had finished all of my course work for my BIS (Bachelor of Independent Studies degree) and I was anxious to begin graduate work as soon as possible.

When I began college, I had hoped very much that after I earned my bachelor's degree, I would be able to attend law school. As I grew more mature, however, this dream began to fade, for there are no law schools in the El Paso area, and I realized that Mother and Dad would never allow me to live on campus for three years at such a young age. Law school, if it ever became a reality, would be a dream I would have to realize as an adult. In the meanwhile, Mother wanted me to continue my education and earn a master's degree, and I, too, was anxious to progress with my studies without a break. Since I had a bachelor's degree in the liberal arts, it seemed natural for me to enroll in a master's program which would emphasize the humanities.

As usual, finding such an institution was easier said than done, but we had fewer difficulties locating a graduate school than we had finding any of our other schools. A classmate of mine had written to me regarding a program offered by the University of the State of New York at Albany, through which a student could supposedly earn a degree without ever setting foot on the university's campus. Although after inquiring we learned that the program was totally unsuitable to our needs, we discovered that the school publishes a catalogue of graduate schools offering external degree programs.

Before I left for my seminars that year we had ordered a copy of this booklet. This time we were anxious to locate an institution with no residency requirements. Attending seminars at BYU had taught us that even a few weeks each year spent away from home can be very expensive and difficult to arrange. Therefore, we automatically disregarded any universities which had "residency requirements" listed in their description. This narrowed the field considerably. Finally, we were down to two which appeared suitable; Norwich University in Vermont, and California State University at Dominguez Hills.

The description under Norwich University stated that the school offered a Master of Liberal Arts degree with no residency requirements. Cal State offered a Master of Arts in the Humanities degree with no residency requirements. I was somewhat inclined toward the former until a friend of ours reminded us that a Master of Liberal Arts degree would contain a much more advanced study of music than I had encountered at BYU. As far as I was concerned, that settled the matter; I had encountered enough difficulties with undergraduate music, and was not at all anxious to repeat the experience. Therefore, we decided to apply to Cal State.

There was only one problem which might complicate my enrollment in another university -- I had not yet officially graduated from BYU. My final grades were in and my studies complete, but I still had to attend two seminars and present my Closure Project before I could graduate.

Since I had to go to BYU for a month during the summer of 1985, Mother told me to ask Dr. Rawson whether he could help us in this matter. Rawson agreed to write a letter of recommendation for me, explaining my current status at BYU and my eligibility for graduate work. He also asked if I had decided where I would be earning my degree. I had to truthfully answer "no" since we had not yet made a final decision. To my surprise, he then recommended California State University at Dominguez Hills stating that BYU was about to implement a graduate external degree program of its own, and that the following autumn he would be taking a tour of universities with such programs. He mentioned that Cal State had a particularly fine program and that BYU would be using it as a model.

Such a glowing recommendation from one of the directors of another institution seemed to be a confirmation that I was supposed to enroll at Cal State. While I was gone, Mother had contacted Dr. Lewis, director of the external degree program at Cal State, inquiring about the program and requesting enrollment forms. Unlike the faculty at Brigham Young University, Dr. Lewis did not seem at all skeptical when he received my initial application.

I received an excellent introduction to my new school. In the letter of recommendation which he wrote to Dr. Lewis, Dr. Rawson stated, "Alexandra Swann has completed the necessary academic work to graduate from Brigham Young University's Bachelor of Independent Study program . . . Officially she will be awarded her diploma in August of 1986, but all of the academic work has been completed which is necessary for graduation . . . Alexandra has been an exceptional student. Her final senior paper on 'Humanism -- America's State Religion?' is one of exceptional, senior level quality. . . She is eligible for graduate work. I recommend her highly to you."

In addition, my grades at BYU had been exemplary -- my final GPA was 3.85. The fact that I had graduated one of the top Western universities with an A average enhanced my credibility and probably eased Cal State's anxieties about my ability to perform well in its program.

Finally, one other event served to firmly establish me at my new school. In September I was finalizing enrollment procedures at Cal State, and by then, Rawson had begun his tour of universities. One afternoon I called Dr. Lewis to ask him a question about my enrollment. When Lewis answered the telephone, he told me that at that moment Jim Rawson was sitting in his office, and that they were discussing me when my call came through. Thus, Dr. Lewis became somewhat familiar with me and my background before I completed my enrollment.

St. Paul commends us in Hebrews to "run with patience the race that is set before us." I had now entered the final leg of my educational race. Cal State would be my last school -- at least for the time being. Therefore, I was anxious to work very hard and earn excellent grades in my M.A. program so that I could finish the academic race as successfully as I had begun it.

In January of the following year, 1986, six months after I had completed my studies at BYU and six months before I would officially receive my diploma, I was contacted by the National Honor Society of Phi Kappa Phi. Although I had not yet graduated, my name had appeared on their list because I had completed my course work and was now enrolled in a graduate program. They wrote: "Your excellent scholastic achievement qualifies you for nomination to membership in the Honor Society of Phi Kappa Phi. . . This invitation represents one of the highest honors the university administration and faculty can bestow on its student scholars. To receive such a nomination is a signal honor."

Information enclosed with the letter stated that Phi Kappa Phi is an honor society as opposed to an honorary society or fraternity. Admission is limited to ten percent or less of a university's graduating class, and requires nomination and approval by a chapter. The society is interdisciplinary and draws membership from all departments within a university, lending diversity to the membership. "Because of their outstanding records, members of Phi Kappa Phi often are preferred candidates for grants, scholarships, and fellowships from institutions where they may continue their education or do research. When they seek jobs, they find their Phi Kappa Phi membership is widely accepted as an indicator of academic ability and motivation."

Of course, I was delighted to receive such an honor, and immediately accepted the invitation. Shortly afterwards, I was contacted by the BYU newspaper, *The Daily Universe* which had learned of my recent induction into the BYU chapter of Phi Kappa Phi and wished to write an article about me. I was interviewed over the telephone, and a few days later the article was published. Unfortunately, the article had inaccurately reported that I had "graduated with honors," though I had not yet graduated at all. I certainly had not made any such statement during the interview, and I do not know why the reporter decided to include it, or even what led her to believe that it was true. Dr. Rawson called me when the article appeared in print (I had not received a copy), and he reaffirmed to me in a note that I would not officially graduate until I had attended my remaining seminars and presented my Closure Project. He was very friendly, and when I explained the circumstances of the interview he told me not to worry about it. The incident seemed to be of little concern to the university, but I was very embarrassed. I was beginning to understand why so many people claim to be misquoted by the press!

The Daily Universe article was not the first which had been done about our family's experience with home-schooling. When Mother and I went to my Foundations seminar, a classmate from California mentioned that she had read about us in a book which had recently been published there. Mother said that she knew nothing about our family having appeared in any book and that Brenda must have us confused with someone else. No, Brenda insisted, the book stated that there was a family in Texas with ten children who were home-schooled and that the oldest child, who was twelve, had just begun her studies at Brigham Young University. We were absolutely incredulous. No one had called us for an interview or to ask us any questions, and yet, from Brenda's description, the information in the book seemed to be accurate. To this day, we have no idea where the author obtained his information.

In the summer of 1985, we received some more conventional publicity when a reporter from the *El Paso Herald Post* asked to interview our family in connection with an article she was doing about home-schooling in the El Paso area. In spite of the fact that our family was across the state line, she wanted to include us in her story.

Two months later, we were again contacted by a reporter, this one from the *El Paso Times*. She read the article in the rival newspaper, and wanted to write an article exclusively about our family. Mother consented, and on a Sunday afternoon, Becky Powers came to our house and conducted a lengthy interview with us. The following week the *Times* sent a photographer to the house who spent about an hour taking photographs of various family members. On Sunday, September 22, 1985, the article appeared on the front page of the newspaper's variety section, and it met with a very positive response.

Mother began to receive letters and phone calls from women she had never met who had read about her in the newspaper. They were housewives who had either been attempting to home-school or had been considering home-schooling but did not know how to begin. Confused and frustrated, they wished to ask the advice of an expert. I believe that Mother could empathize with their situations, and she never failed to return their inquiries. Although her own schedule was (and is) incredibly hectic she always took the time to try to help a fellow home-schooler get on his feet.

What surprised us even more than the immediate response from the local area, however, was the mail we received from other areas. We have been contacted by several families in Arizona who have read articles about us. One of these families even came to visit us on their way to Carlsbad, New Mexico. For the longest time we could not understand where so many Arizona families were hearing about us, though we had noticed that all of those who contacted us were LDS, and we wondered if perhaps our connection with BYU had something to do with this instant celebrity. Finally, we discovered that the *Latter Day Sentinel* had published a brief article about me taken from the article in the *Daily Universe*.

We also received a great deal of response from the Dallas area after Mother testified at *Leeper vs. Arlington* in January of 1987. We assumed that most of the people contacting us had heard of her because of her testimony, but recently a woman from that area sent Mother a copy of a Dallas article about us. It turned out to be the *El Paso Times* article rewritten. Still, it seems odd to learn for the first time that one has appeared in articles for which he has not even been interviewed.

Not long ago, Mother was talking to a woman who had been her neighbor for several years before my parents had any children. The woman's son, who is now attending college in Dallas, had been researching a paper on home-schooling when he ran across an article about our family which he used as a source for his paper. He added a personal note in relating our experiences by ending the segment with, "I grew up next door to these people."

As my Closure seminar drew to an end, I reflected on these and all of the other events which had taken place during my years at BYU. I had many sweet memories of my school, and several less-than-sweet ones, but I knew that above all else the years there had been well spent. When at last the final day of the Closure seminar arrived, I was ready to say an emotional as well as a verbal goodbye. Thursday morning the last presentations were made, and then most of the students went upstairs to attend the graduation banquet.

Commencement ceremonies would take place the following day. I had already determined that I did not wish to stay for either the banquet or the ceremonies. Dad had been forced to be out of town at the same time that we were, and Christopher, who was fourteen, and Francesca, who was thirteen, had been left to look after the smaller children while everyone was away. Although a friend of my parents' was checking on them everyday, Mother and I both felt that it would be best to hurry home as quickly as possible. In graduating I had closed a very important chapter in my life, and I was anxious to enter the era which lay before me.

During my three years at BYU I had done well on every test. With my graduation, I felt a sense of relief because I believed that my years of agonizing through exams were behind me. Yet, only nine months later I would face the most difficult, nerve-wracking test of my life -- my driver's test. At last the long awaited, highly coveted driver's license was within my reach.

"Never go near the water until you learn to swim," my grandfather used to caution his children. After a few months of driving lessons I was prepared to create my own version of that saying, "Never get behind the wheel of a car until you learn how to drive."

Actually, my first driving experience occurred when I was only two years old. My father left me in the car just long enough for him to dash into the post office and pick up our mail. Those few moments were also just long enough for me to put the car in gear and roll down an incline, broadsiding a brand new Cadillac. The owner, a male nurse, was hysterical. My father was aghast. I remained perfectly calm as I told the police officer, "It's all my daddy's fault." Little did I know as I sat there innocently sucking my thumb that my first experience behind the wheel was a portent of things to come.

As I matured, like most children I dreamed of the day when, driver's license in hand, I would "put the pedal to the metal" and sail down the freeway with my radio blaring and my hair flying in the wind, but when the time came for my first lesson, I was brutally confronted with harsh reality. Mother had elected to let me make my debut in our fourteen-year-old Volkswagen van. She stopped on the shoulder of the road, put on the emergency brake, and then allowed me to take control. After turning the key and shifting into first gear, I naively expected the car to roll forward as it had for Mother. Unfortunately, my vehicle was unwilling to be so cooperative. After traveling a distance of about ten feet the van's engine died. I started it again, put my foot on the accelerator, and traveled about five more feet before the engine again died. By this time I had become totally frustrated -- obviously, the vehicle had some mechanical fault which had not become apparent until I took the driver's seat. Upon close examination, however, I found that I had forgotten one of the most basic rules of driving -- to release the emergency brake. From that moment I knew that my vehicle and I were not going to be friends.

After months of having me practice on dirt roads which stretched from nowhere to nowhere, Mother decided that in order to hone my driving skills I needed to obtain a learner's permit and drive in traffic. Anxious to pass the test, I first sent for a copy of the state driver's manual and studied it diligently. Then the day arrived when I found myself standing at the end of a long line directed by three obese, snarling civil servants in a small, dingy building which served as the headquarters of the Department of Motor Vehicles. Clutching my birth certificate, I timidly stepped forward as one woman barked at me to enter the testing room and then slapped a pencil and a test down on the desk in front of me. My apprehensions soon disappeared -- I aced the written test and the eye test was a piece of cake.

As I confidently slipped into the driver's seat of my father's brand new T-Bird with my learner's permit in hand, I felt better than I had in months. Driving wasn't going to be nearly so difficult as I had thought. I could feel my chest swelling with pride as I confidently swung into the driveway. "Stop!" my mother cried frantically. Too late, I had already hit the semi-circular rock wall, devastating the car's front bumper. The euphoria instantly dissolved into a sinking feeling as I contemplated a means of leaving the country before my father got home that night.

Within a few weeks I was back on the road following a stern

reprimand from Dad. Although I was greatly comforted by Mother's gentle assurances that, "It will get easier," I still found driving to be a most difficult and frustrating activity.

Finally, the day arrived for me to take my road test and I returned to the small, dingy building. In an emotionless monotone, the traffic officer, who more resembled a robot than a policeman, ordered me to get into the car. "I'll tell you what to do," he stated without expression, and he then asked me if I had any questions.

The only question I wanted to ask was, "Why do you talk like that?" but fearing that this would only alienate him, I kept quiet. After demonstrating all the car's gadgets I began to cautiously creep around the block. I had safely completed all of the necessary maneuvers, and was feeling a little more relaxed when the officer instructed me to parallel park. I meekly asked if I could skip this part of the test, promising to never attempt to parallel park in real life. He told me that if I attempted and failed I could still get my license but that if I refused even to try he would be forced to fail me for the entire test.

As beads of perspiration appeared on my forehead, I struggled to remember the exact maneuvers outlined for this procedure in the driver's manual. Two minutes later I drove away from the parallel parking area leaving behind two orange pancakes where the markers had previously stood. As I pulled into the parking area of the Department of Motor Vehicles, I wondered if the officer would arrest me, or merely let me off with a fine. To my amazement he said, "Go inside and they will give you a temporary license which you can use until your permanent one arrives from Santa Fe."

That evening at the dinner table I was ecstatic as I proudly displayed my license and bored the family with every detail of the test. "Any fool can learn to drive," Christopher quipped. Easy for him to say; he seems to be able to make the great gas-guzzling beasts obey his every whim. As for me, I have come to the conclusion that it is not so much a matter of driving as of being driven. Upon closing the door and putting on my seat belt, I invariably find myself trapped inside a technological terror which delights in speeding, running red lights, and causing me other forms of misery. Further, I have noticed that no matter where I want to go, my car always wants to go somewhere else, and a veritable battle of the wills ensues, of which I am generally the loser.

Gone are my childhood fantasies. A blaring radio would be much too distracting from the intense concentration necessary for me to back out of the driveway. Hair cannot fly when it is carefully covered by a crash helmet, color coordinated to go with my matching asbestos body suit. As for sailing down the freeway, why they won't even let you on the freeway when you refuse to drive above thirty-five miles per hour.

EIGHT
ANNUIT COEPTIS
"GOD HAS FAVORED OUR UNDERTAKING"

By the time of my graduation from Brigham Young University, I had been a student at California State University for almost a year. In fact, I was nearing the completion of my studies at Cal State, and was actually in the process of writing my master's thesis. My year with my new school had already been most unique and interesting.

I soon discovered that Cal State was as far removed from BYU as graduate work is from undergraduate. When I enrolled in the program I had the choice of completing "Curriculum A" or "Curriculum B." Curriculum A was more of a liberal arts program and required that the student take courses in a variety of subjects including art and music. Curriculum B was much more specialized, allowing the student to concentrate upon three out of five possible areas of study. From among the disciplines of history, music, art, literature, and philosophy a student could choose one major and two minors.

For me this was a totally new experience, for at BYU I had not had a major. Mother and I decided upon Curriculum B, and I chose, at her suggestion, to major in history and minor in philosophy and literature. History has always been one of my favorite subjects. Although I had taken some history in every school I had attended, nothing compared to my study of history at Cal State. At BYU I studied history, but the course was devoted mainly to the study of "historical perspective" rather than historical events. Yet, the course did prove to be helpful because it acquainted me with the methods and mentality of the historian.

At Cal State history seemed to be an entirely new discipline. One of the first courses I took was a study of Carnegie, Rockefeller, and Ford, and how their ideas and practices created the modern day work force. Among the books I was assigned were *Robber Barons* by Matthew Josephson, and *Labor and Monopoly Capital* by Harry Braverman. I was fascinated by *Robber Barons,* for it contained wonderful anecdotes about the constant feuds between the great capitalists of the late 1800's and early 1900's.

During my first semester I also took a philosophy course which focused on Voltaire and Rousseau. Since I knew almost nothing about either of these men, I greatly enjoyed this course as well. I was assigned Rosseau's *Confessions* and the *Creed of the Savoyard Priest,* and Voltaire's *Candide,* and my writing assignments included discussions of their respective philosophies. The course also served to rekindle my interest in France -- an interest I have had since I was a very small child. Later I would merge my love for history and my fascination with France into one colossal project.

The following semester I took "Defining the Humanities: History," a required course which focused primarily on "historical mindedness" rather than actual events. The course taught me not to take everything in a history book at "face value," to look for the underlying causes of the events described, and to recognize and acknowledge the prejudices of the "experts."

Aside from the curriculum, Cal State was a new experience in other ways. For the first time I was on a semester system. In my other schools, a student could enroll at any time of the year, and he could complete his studies at his own pace. At Cal State one could enroll only at the beginning of the semester, and then he could sign up for only as many courses as he could complete during the fifteen week semester.

Each course had its own course guide, in which the professor provided background information about the course and the assignments and outlined the semester for the student. He might assign the first paper to be submitted during Week III, the second might be due Week XI and the final written assignment due Week XV.

At first I had a difficult time adjusting to this schedule. During my first term at the university the bookstore sent my books four weeks late -- even though I had ordered them well before the semester began. My first assignments were due Week V and I was desperate to have them in on time. I knew that the school frowned on tardiness, and I wanted to commence my work on the right footing. Thursday afternoon the books finally arrived, and knowing that my papers were due the following week, I worked all weekend reading hundreds of pages. By the first of the week I had written each of my first two papers and submitted them to my professors with a note of apology for having mailed them just under the deadline. Dr. Lewis, who was the philosophy professor as well as the administrator of the program, sent back a note saying that my philosophy paper had been the first to arrive at the school!

Although the schedule caused me a few headaches during the first term, as I became accustomed to it, I found that it actually made my life much easier. There were only a certain number of units I could take in one semester and still be finished before it ended. Most courses were three units, though the Defining the Humanities courses were 2 units each. Therefore, Mother usually enrolled me in three 3 unit courses or one 2 unit course and two 3 unit courses per semester.

I sometimes had two papers due the same week, but more often I would have a paper from one course due the third week, a paper from another course due the fifth, and a paper from a third course due the seventh week. Mother had me mark an appointment calendar to show each week of the term and the due date of each of my assignments. I knew exactly how much work I had to do each day in order to have my papers ready on time, and I did only that amount. I knew that I could easily read a four hundred page book in two weeks, and that I could easily write a seven to ten page paper in one week.

I found that, on the average, my assignments were a little longer than they had been at BYU. Many required that I write papers from five to seven pages in length. A few assignments called for papers between three to five pages in length, but assignments calling for seven to ten page papers were not unusual. The content of these papers was also different. Graduate work required a great deal more analysis and in-depth discussion than I had been accustomed to at the undergraduate level.

Yet, my own school day actually decreased. Instead of coming to school at eight-thirty each morning and breaking at ten-thirty I now started at nine-thirty and worked until eleven-thirty. In the past, I had always worked at least three hours a day. At Cal State I worked an average of between two and two and a half hours a day. Often I did not come back in the afternoon at all, and when I did I generally did not work very long. Even so, I nearly always finished the semester at least a week or two in advance of the closing date.

Aside from my reduced school day, I often had three to four weeks off between semesters, and I enjoyed the breaks from studying, for I had worked summer and winter for ten years. Mother put my vacations to good use, however. She assigned me odd jobs to do about the house and often had me help her teach the younger children some of their assignments. One month she set me to work typing Christopher's and Francesca's assignments for BYU.

By the time that I began Cal State in 1985, Mother had seven children in school, and Gabrielle was about to begin. Christopher would be finishing BYU in one year, and Francesca had about two years left. The other children were either in grade school or high school. Just keeping abreast of everyone's schedule was exhausting. Often Mother's schoolday did not end until three or four P.M. Much had changed since the days when I was in Calvert. Now, instead of having to prepare one child for a test, she might have to prepare two or three at a time. She was constantly monitoring all of her students, and she continued to personally supervise the smaller children's lessons. Even during the times when I helped her, she was always present in the classroom and kept a watchful eye on us.

I now needed less supervision than ever before, but Mother continued to take an active role in my studies. She still read every text assigned to me, and every morning she asked me what I was doing in school. Often she looked at my lessons herself, though she was learning to trust my ability and judgment more and more. Now, it was not uncommon for me to read a book, write a paper, and then type it without her ever having seen my assignment. However, she always read my papers before they were mailed to the school. One reason that she allowed me more freedom was because of my grades -- I carried a 4.0 during my first two semesters at Cal State.

Although my hours were shorter, I felt that I was getting more from my study sessions than ever before. There are certain elements for which a professor looks as he grades a student's writing, and I had learned to employ those elements in my work. I had learned how to find the critical points and arguments in a lengthy book and to comment upon them in a critical, intelligent manner.

During my second semester at Cal State I took a philosophy course entitled "Biblical Movement," under William Hagan. The course focused upon three different views of the Bible. I read a number of commentaries on the book of Jonah and was then assigned a paper on the Fundamentalist, Liberal and Humanist interpretations of the book. I had a similar assignment for the New Testament. My assignment on the book of Jonah was returned to me with an AB, which is Cal State's equivalent of an A—, and a note from my professor saying that I could bring it up to a full A by doing a little additional work on the assignment and returning it to him. Delighted to have the opportunity to improve my grade, I gladly made the changes. I earned an A for the paper and an A for the course.

Another philosophy course I took under Dr. Lewis was entitled "The Evolution of Human Culture." As a part of my assignments I read Sophocles' *Antigone*, Plato's *The Republic, The Song of Roland*, B.F. Skinner's *Waldon Two*, and Thomas More's *Utopia*. After each of these readings I was required to write essays reflecting my comprehension of the ideas and central arguments.

Naturally, I was enthused about being involved in such an interesting program, and I enjoyed sharing some of the aspects of my work with my family. Of course, Mother was already well aware of my assignments, for she was reading my books and looking over my finished essays with me, but I loved to sit at the dinner table and tell the other members of the family -- especially Dad -- about every aspect of my studies. Most of the time he was incredibly patient, and after coming in exhausted from a difficult day at work he would listen politely while I chattered ceaselessly about books I happened to be reading or papers I happened to be writing.

Sometimes, however, even he reached his limits. Once Christopher and I were enrolled in a philosophy course which *required that we read Zen and the Art of Motorcycle Maintenance* by Robert Pirsig. Of course, mother was reading it also, and for days the three of us talked of nothing but the book. After a few evenings, Dad informed us that he would be delighted when we finished the course so that we could stop reading the book, but in the meantime he hoped very much that none of us would feel compelled to mention it to him again because he could not stand to hear any more about Pirsig's philosophy. We obediently honored the request and henceforth discussed *Zen* only among ourselves.

Most of the time he seemed to enjoy hearing about my work, however, and I, in turn, enjoyed hearing about his. Since Dad was always willing to become involved in my projects, it seemed only fair that sooner or later I should become involved in one of his. My opportunity arrived shortly before my sixteenth birthday. The year that Dad was working in El Paso for the Houston based corporation, he assisted with the campaign of a candidate for Congressman. The campaign officials needed volunteers to stick address labels on prestuffed envelopes, and Dad immediately offered the services of Christopher, Francesca, Dominic and me. His colleagues were supposed to arrange for the services of fourteen additional volunteers.

Mother gave us a day off from school for a good cause, and Dad had us outside the proper building at the stroke of ten A.M., the time on which they had agreed. Unfortunately, the person who was supposed to open the doors had not yet arrived. After waiting until past ten-thirty, Dad, who had to return to work, but did not wish to leave us standing outside the locked building for an indefinite period of time, drove us to his office. He told us to sit down while he called to learn where the problem lay. He was told that the building would not be open until two o'clock that afternoon, and that we would have to wait until then.

Dad brought us each a Coke and admonished us to keep quiet until noon when he would take us to lunch. He then hurried off to attend to his business. I felt as though I were five years old again, for it had been many years since the old "lunches out" with Dad. At noon he took us to an Italian restaurant and bought us a delicious meal. He then drove us back to the building, which by then was open.

The four of us entered, immediately noticing that no other volunteers were present. A woman showed us how to begin, and we settled down to work. Never have we observed two hours of such unbroken silence. We did not laugh, or even speak to each other, except to occasionally mention an acquaintance whose name appeared on the mailing labels. In the Swann tradition we were organized -- Mother would have been proud to see the division of labor which occurred naturally among us. Christopher, Dominic, and I put the labels on the envelopes, and Francesca sorted them according to zip code, bound them together with rubber bands and put them in small bags. Once the woman who had shown us into the building came in and pasted on a few labels -- probably not more than fifty. A little later another woman joined us briefly. The rest of the time we worked completely alone.

At four o'clock the attendant told us to call our father and tell him to pick us up because she had to leave at four-thirty. Dad could not leave at that precise moment, and he told me to ask her to stay until he arrived. We continued to work until he walked through the door. The attendant estimated that we had stamped about five thousand envelopes in two and one half hours. If she were correct, we each stamped approximately 1250 envelopes in 150 minutes, or over eight envelopes per minute.

I continued to study summer and winter, taking vacations only at holidays or during breaks between semesters. However, I did not find such a schedule tiring and was content to work year round even as I became older.

I always thought that I had an unusually good attitude about my schedule until my brother Christopher began the program one year after I did. Although I had never complained about not having more free time, I always took advantage of whatever free time I did have. I looked forward to the breaks between semesters, and I assumed that my siblings would also. To my surprise, Christopher, who claimed to enjoy school a great deal less than I, spent more time working at it. Rather than taking breaks between semesters, he spent his free time preparing the next semester's assignments. Mother constantly asked him if he would not like to take an afternoon off since he was so far ahead, but he always replied, "No, I think I'll work." For several semesters he had his assignments completed before the term even began, and he then spent the semester doing the following semester's work.

At Cal State thirty units are required for graduation from the Master of Arts program. Consequently, it was not long before I was nearing the midpoint in the program, and the time had arrived for me to choose a subject for my Independent Study work.

Cal State's program is designed so that the student is required to take a certain number of Independent Study courses in the area of his major. With the help of his professor, he designs his own curriculum based on a subject of particular interest to him. The professor approves the suggested topic and also a book list and specified number of written assignments as submitted by the student. The student and his mentor sign a contract stating the exact number and nature of the papers which will be expected from the student and the contract "goes into effect" until the end of the semester.

Independent Study courses are three units each and include 15-20 pages of written material divided into whatever number of papers on which the student and his professor agree. They are to include the use of both primary and secondary sources -- primary sources being those written during the period being researched or by the individual being studied, and secondary sources being historical works written after the event -- and are intended to represent careful scholarly work. Independent Study is an excellent addition to the program because it allows the student to research extensively subjects about which he himself has a deep interest but might never explore otherwise.

When the time came for me to begin my Independent Study work, Mother realized that this would be an excellent opportunity for me to do background work for my master's thesis. My subjects for my Independent Study units should, therefore, be related to the subject on which I would write my thesis. Of course, since my major was history, both my thesis and my Independent Study assignments would also be related to history. While we were discussing this, she suddenly asked me on what subject I would like to write my master's thesis. I actually had given absolutely no thought to either my thesis or a possible topic and was caught unawares. Out of the "clear blue sky" I announced that I wanted to write my thesis on the French Revolution. Mother did not object and proposed that I should devote my Independent Study units to events leading up to the revolution. She suggested France's role in the American Revolution for the first three unit course.

Accordingly, I submitted my topic along with a complete outline and a booklist of both primary and secondary sources to be used in writing the paper. Upon receiving permission from my mentor to begin, I proceeded to write my first eight to ten page paper on France's role in the American Revolution. My second eight to ten page paper concentrated on the effect of the American Revolution on the psyche of France, and explained how French involvement in our Revolution may have prepared them for their own uprising.

My next independent study concentrated on the state of pre-revolutionary France. I wrote one five to seven page paper on the moral and social climate of the country, one paper on the nation's economic state, and one paper on France's political climate just prior to the Revolution.

Although I knew that I wanted to write my thesis on some

aspect of the French Revolution, I had not given any thought to a specific focus. In fact, I did not know enough about my subject to decide upon a particular topic. I went to the library and selected some books on Revolutionary France from the card catalogue. During one of my readings I came across a reference to the Committee of Public Safety, but at the time the name meant little to me. As I read further, however, I became intrigued by every aspect of the Revolution from the king to the sans culottes. Most fascinating by far were the leaders of the Revolution -- Robesierre, Marat, and Danton -- and the revolutionary government they established. I found a wealth of information in the BYU library, and I spent six weeks reading and taking notes.

Of course, common sense should have suggested that "The French Revolution" was much too broad a topic for a sixty page thesis, but as it turned out, this observation was left to be made by Dr. Rowley's wife. While I was researching the thesis we had the opportunity to discuss my topic, and Mrs. Rowley asked on what specific aspect of the Revolution I had chosen to focus. I told her that I had not yet decided, but I was considering writing the paper as a broad overview of the period. Mrs. Rowley correctly pointed out that volumes have been written on the subject, and that I would have to narrow my topic enough to effectively deal with it in a relatively short space. She also mentioned that I would have to choose a unique aspect of the period -- a topic upon which not much has been written. "Why don't you do something about the women of the French Revolution?" she suggested.

I realized that she was right, but I did not care for her suggestion of a topic. I was much too enamored with the villains of the revolution to be terribly interested in its women. A day or two later I received a letter from Dr. Howard Holter, my mentor for the project. He asked for a working outline of the thesis, a tentative booklist, and some sample pages. He, too, had mentioned that the topic of the paper would have to be narrowed considerably. Because I would have to be able to justify my thesis as an original work, my topic would also have to be original. I promised Mother that I would quickly decide on a focus.

I knew that I simply would not be content with the thesis unless I could focus it largely upon Robespierre, Marat and Danton. In my research I had come across numerous references to the Jacobin Club, a social meeting house for the revolutionaries which later became the most powerful club in France and the virtual seat of government during the

Revolution. As all three of my subjects were members, I decided that a study of the clubs would be the ideal focus. I immediately informed Mother that I would be writing my thesis on "The Jacobins."

Although the French Revolution is one of the most significant events of the eighteenth century, few Americans know very much about it. Sources on the Jacobins are particularly difficult to find because not much has been written about the clubs, and that which has usually addresses only one aspect of the institutions, such as organization and policy. I would be bringing together in one work many different aspects of the clubs and would be focusing largely on three of their most famous members -- Maximilien Robespierre, Georges Danton, and Jean Paul Marat. I would trace the clubs from their inception in 1789 to their demise in 1794 and would explore the methods they used to gain and wield their power. The paper would be unique in that it would be incorporating into one work information which could previously be discovered only by consulting a variety of sources.

Unfortunately, the very aspects which made the paper so easy to justify made it extremely difficult to write. I found it almost impossible to locate the information I needed, not only to actually write the paper, but even to gain a sufficient understanding of the relationships of the various people and associations so that I could reconcile their positions in my own mind. In addition, I was operating under another handicap. I do not read French; consequently, all of my sources had to be in English. I did not have a problem accumulating secondary sources -- historical studies -- but primary sources were a different matter. Many of the best of the French primary sources do not appear to have been translated, and I did not have access to those which have been. This brought me to a second dilemma; most sources written in English at the time of the French Revolution were authored by the English, who often had a negative view of the events taking place in France. Therefore, I had to be careful that my sources did not display an obvious bias.

Rosseau and Revolution by Will and Ariel Durant, was a tremendous help to me in providing the background information I needed to explain the circumstances leading up to the events of 1789. David Jordan's *The Revolutionary Career of Maximilien Robespierre* contained a fascinating portrait of the infamous leader which would provide some of the information I would need to write a brief profile of "The Incorruptible." Clarence Brinton's *The Jacobins,* from which I took the title for my own work, provided valuable information on the organization and strategies of the clubs. Stanley Loomis' *Paris in the Terror,* which contained information about the political power of the Jacobins, provided an excellent source on the violence of the Reign of Terror and wonderful insight into the minds of the revolutionaries.

In addition to these and other secondary sources, I found four reputable primary ones -- Arthur Young's *Travels in France During the Years 1787, 1788, 1789,* John Moore's *A Journal During a Residence in France,* Grace Elliot's *During the Reign of Terror,* and Jean Jacques Rousseau's *On the Social Contract.* Rosseau's work was written prior to the revolution, but since many of the goals of the revolutionaries had been based on his ideas, he proved to be a valuable source. I was fortunate -- although all of my sources were in English, only two of the authors were British, and the other two were French. All of the works were cited by historians as reputable sources of information. Yet, my difficulties with the paper were far from being resolved. My thesis could be between 4 and 6 units, with each unit being the equivalent of ten pages of written work. I needed six units in order to graduate; therefore, my thesis would have to be sixty pages in length. My problem was not in making the thesis long enough, however, but in condensing the material I had into that short a space. Remembering the three rewrites of my Closure Project at BYU, I was determined not to submit this paper until I felt certain that it could be accepted on the first draft. I wrote the initial draft but was very unhappy with the result; it was too vague and did not delve deeply enough into the subject of the Jacobins. I tore up most of it, keeping only my introduction and a few passages which I felt were worth salvaging. In its next draft, the paper was 110 pages and dragged at points. "Totally unsatisfactory," I told myself, and most of this draft saw the wastebasket also.

By now I was getting desperate. I needed to finish the paper before the end of the winter semester in order to graduate in May, and I had only a few weeks left. Frantic, I began to write a third draft. Page after page flew out of the typewriter as I combined the best of my first two attempts with new material. At last I felt satisfied. My final draft contained all the elements I felt should be employed. Mother read it as I typed it, and she pronounced it "excellent."

In order to make certain that the paper would not be sent back because of improper form, at the time I began working on the project I had sent for a copy of the university's style guide and had also purchased a copy of Kate Turabian's *Manual for Writers' of Theses and Dissertations.* Because our typewriter was old and produced poor quality work, Dad agreed to retype my final draft on a typewriter at his office. Evening after evening, he stayed late and typed the pages I had given him that morning. I was very grateful to him, for by the time he had typed the entire text, which was seventy-two pages, plus the nineteen pages of endnotes, the two page bibliography, the table of contents, the cover page, the abstract, and the preface, he had typed over one hundred pages of material. He did a wonderful job -- the paper looked very professional. Though I knew he must have been delighted when I mailed the project to the school and he no longer had to work on it after office hours, he never complained about the extra effort and always praised the thesis warmly.

One week before Christmas, 1986, I mailed the paper to the school, hoping desperately that after all of the time and effort we had spent, Dr. Holter would accept it on the first submission. I was tired even of the sight of it, and I am certain that the rest of the family was equally tired of hearing me discuss it. I had spent four months writing my thesis -- longer than I had ever spent on any other single project. The work had been complicated, difficult, and exhausting. I did not feel that I could bear to rewrite it, although, of course, I would if the professor insisted. About a month later, Dr. Holter returned the thesis to me. He had accepted it with a grade of 97/A and would require no revisions. I felt wonderful!

During my last semester at Cal State, I enrolled in one final course on France -- not an Independent Study, but a course designed by Dr. Holter entitled "The Age of Revolution." I enrolled partially because I had already done a tremendous amount of research on the subject, and I hoped that I would not have to work very hard. I was wrong -- I had not read any of the books assigned by Dr. Holter in my other research, and I was dealing with many new concepts. Still, the background I already had helped somewhat.

I believe that I enjoyed that course more than any other I took at Cal State. As one of my assignments I was instructed to read Dicken's *A Tale of Two Cities* and write a paper contrasting the views of one of the historical studies assigned in the course to that of Dickens. Although I had read the book once several years before, it is one of my favorite fictional works, and I welcomed the chance to read it again. As always, Mother and I discussed the paper before I wrote it, and she was able to give me helpful insights. When the paper was returned to me, Dr. Holter had marked it 99/A+. Regarding my comment that much can be learned about the revolution from reading both Dickens' novel and a historical work, Holter had written, "I'm glad you think so, considering the work you yourself have done on The Rev." I was delighted, for I felt that both the course and the grade had been a very nice conclusion to a wonderful eighteen months spent earning my M.A.

In May of 1987 I graduated. Although I had finished my studies in April, the ceremonies were not held until the following month. I did not attend; thus, it was several months before I received my diploma, but I felt as exuberant as any other graduate. Mother, too, felt a sense of accomplishment. Horatius had at last triumphed at the bridge. Of course, the battle was not completely over -- there were still nine other students remaining to progress through their studies, but now things would be different. The schools had been located; the groundwork had been laid. She had proven herself capable of tutoring her children at home, without help. As she expressed it at the time of my graduation, "I have seen the first fruits of my labors." In spite of the skepticism and criticism with which their ideas had met, my parents had proven that it is not impossible to tutor ten children at home with exceptional results. In a sense, my graduation was a victory for all of us.

Graduation gave me an opportunity to reflect on the past eleven years. Annuit Coeptis is a phrase which seems to summarize our experiences -- in Latin it means "God has favored our undertaking." God had, indeed, blessed our efforts with success. I had spent many years of hard work, but in looking back I could see that it had been worthwhile. My experiences with home-schooling had been very positive ones -- I had truly enjoyed school. Even projects such as completing the music course at BYU and writing my master's thesis had been very good for me. I had developed a sense of confidence in my own ability to work through difficult and complex problems.

Immediately after graduation I felt very tired, and almost a little burned out. I was grateful, therefore, to be able to take several months off after eleven years of almost continuous study. The break gave me an opportunity to help Mother with some of the other children. I gained a new appreciation for the amount of time and effort she had put into this program. I also could relate to the children better than ever before. A sense of nostalgia came over me as I watched them studying, for I remembered how I felt at their ages. I understood their impatience for the day to arrive when they, too, would finish school. Yet, I knew that they enjoyed learning and could not imagine life without school.

Whatever my future may hold, I have my education. At the age of sixteen I graduated with a GPA of 3.84 and a Master of Arts in the Humanities Degree from California State University. No matter what else may happen, I will never lose the knowledge that I have gained, and that is a very nice feeling. To me, the work and effort have been worthwhile -- summer vacations for a master's degree in my mid-teens is, in my estimation, a fair trade. If I had the opportunity to do so, I would not alter even one aspect of my education or my upbringing, for I feel that they could not have been improved.

Most parents hope to leave their children something on which to depend when they reach adulthood. My parents have given me the legacy of a good education and a respect for proper values. It is a legacy which will serve me through the remainder of my life, for unlike money or other possessions, knowledge lasts a lifetime. My upbringing has been very unusual in some ways, but, in my opinion, it is the unusual aspects which have made it most rewarding. I cannot claim that it is a lifestyle which would be best for everyone; I can only say that I have no regrets.

AFTERWARD

Dear Parent,

   I frequently receive telephone calls from men and women from all parts of this country who are either considering home-schooling or are already involved in a home study program. These parents nearly always express some apprehensions about embarking on such an ambitious undertaking, and over the years I have found that the questions are nearly always the same: How can I insure that my child will really learn all that he needs to prepare him for admittance to a good university? How can I be certain that I have chosen the best curriculum for my child? How can I teach my child subjects which I never took in school or in which I did poorly? And finally, the most asked question of all -- how can I take on the job of educating my child at home and still have time to take care of my responsibilities as a wife and mother?

   First, I want to make it clear that I do not have all the answers. But, I have been home-schooling for nearly fourteen years, and I have been faced with the same problems that other home-schooling parents encounter. In fact, because I have home-schooled ten children, it is probably fair to say that I have had to deal with more problems than most home-schooling parents. That is why I want to take this opportunity to share with you some of the lessons that I have learned that make home-schooling not only a means of education but possibly the best form of education available in today's world.

How can you be sure that your child will receive an education which will prepare him for university work? Actually, in a home-schooling situation you can do far more to insure that your child is learning than you can in any other circumstance.

We Americans are so specialized that we tend to believe that only an "expert" is capable of performing tasks that for centuries were not considered fields of specialization. For instance, until the second half of this century, if we became ill we called our family doctor. He arrived at our door with his little black bag and called us by our first names as he dispensed pills and ointments to cure our ills. He didn't have us fill out a form giving our medical history because he already knew it. He delivered our babies and set our broken bones. He nursed us through mumps and measles and assured us that everything was going to be just fine -- and usually he was right.

Then came specialization and the "family doctor" went the way of the dinosaur and the carrier pigeon. He grew old and died and there was no one to replace him. Yes, there were lots of fine young doctors, but none of them treated the whole person. If you had an earache you consulted Dr. Jones, but you did not dare ask him about your infected toe -- that was Dr. Smith's specialty. So it happened that while medical care may have improved in some respects, in the process we lost a friend who really did care about us personally, and who usually was just as able to meet our needs as his specializing counterpart.

Much the same thing has happened with education. Home-schooling is not new -- it is the oldest method of teaching. Our country was made great by men and women who were taught at home (or in the home-like environment of a one-room school). The teacher in the New England or Middle colony may not have been an "expert" in every field, but she knew the children in her small school, and it was not unusual for a child to receive all of his formal education from the same teacher. In the South, children were commonly tutored in their homes and usually did not attend school until they went to England to enter the university. Yet, it is fair to say that the level of education that existed in this country during our early years was superior to that which exists today.

138

Oh yes, we have teachers who are probably better equipped to teach a single subject than the parent or country school teacher of old, but again, we have lost the personal contact so necessary in dealing with the whole individual. I am not laying the fault at the feet of the teachers -- many of them are dedicated individuals who are doing the best they can. They, too, are victims of the system. But the fact is that your child deserves something better. He deserves a teacher who loves him more than anyone in the world. He deserves a teacher who wants the best for him educationally, spiritually, and emotionally. He deserves a teacher who wants to watch him grow into a sound and happy individual who will be an asset to society. In short, your child deserves to have you as his teacher.

You can provide your child with the tools he needs in order to do well in any university. You can teach him basics in English and mathematics; you can acquaint him with the world around him through texts in science and geography; you can help him to understand himself and his neighbors through the study of history and literature. But -- most important of all -- you can teach your child to love learning, and the child who loves learning will continue to learn long after his formal education has ended.

After a parent makes the decision to home-school, she is faced with the problem of locating a suitable curriculum, and frequently it is at this point that the home-school runs into problems. Home-schooling parents tend to haunt book fairs, book sales, and book stores. They often purchase more materials than they need or materials that they later discover are unsuited to their needs. In the process they may neglect certain areas of study altogether. Because educational materials are expensive, these parents may be dismayed to discover that after spending hundred of dollars they are still not satisfied that they have put together a comprehensive course of study.

That is why I urge parents to take advantage of one of the courses which has been designed especially for this purpose. In our home we use Calvert School for grades one through eight and the American School for grades nine through twelve, but there are a number of other excellent courses on the market which offer a variety of approaches to home-study. These programs are constantly updated to insure that the child is being taught a comprehensive program with current information that is appropriate for his grade level. I believe that because these programs usually make it unnecessary to purchase additional materials, they are nearly always less expensive than a program which is designed by the parent.

The key here is to shop around. Call or write to schools offering correspondence courses and find out exactly what they offer. Ask questions: Is the course accredited? Does it include everything that the child needs to complete a particular grade level? What does the accrediting association have to say about the program? How long has the program been in existence? Can a child progress at his own pace? Will the school provide assistance if you experience a problem?

Most parents who begin a home-school fear that as their children enter high school they will be unable to continue their role as teacher. What these parents do not realize is that they will learn along with their children. Like it or not, the home-schooling parent relearns every grade level, and by the time her child is ready to progress to the next grade, so is she!

As she teaches her child, the parent relearns the most basic principles of mathematics. One day that parent discovers a concept that is new to her, but because she has rebuilt her math foundation, she is able to quickly grasp the new material. Soon the parent is thoroughly familiar with this principle, and it has now become part of her math foundation. In this way a parent can continue, almost indefinitely, to educate herself while educating her child. In high school, when algebra and geometry are introduced, the parent is not suddenly faced with a terrifying maze of unintelligible equations -- as the new concepts are introduced, she simply adds them to her own foundation and then passes them on to her child.

If this sounds difficult, it isn't, but it does require that a parent takes the time to prepare herself for her role as teacher. The best way to do this is to read each day's lessons ahead of time and make certain that she thoroughly understands the material herself. This may mean less time spent in front of the television set, but many parents find these learning sessions challenging and stimulating.

Finally, most mothers fear that if they become involved in a home-school, they will not have time for their families or themselves. While it is true that teaching eight or ten children is extremely time consuming, it is also true that teaching one or two is not. Most parents can expect to spend no more than three hours each day in the classroom, and that leaves ample time for household chores and other activities. It is also important to remember that the fewer children that are involved, the less the preparation time will be.

It is imperative, though, to set aside regular hours and adhere to them religiously. Parents must decide on a schedule that suits their family's lifestyle and STICK TO IT. Consistency is absolutely crucial to success, but with careful planning and unwavering commitment, almost anyone can have a successful program.

If you are considering home-schooling your children, I hope that Alexandra's narrative has inspired you to make a commitment. If you are already home-schooling, I trust that *No Regrets* has encouraged you to push onward toward that day when you will see your children complete their educations and become part of the oldest of all alumni -- that vast body of students that reaches back to Isaiah and stretches forward to infinity -- the universal school of home-educated students.

Best wishes,

Joyce Swann